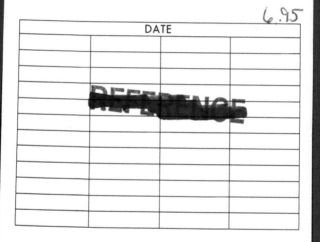

TWAYNE'S WORLD AUTHORS SERIES

A Survey of the World's Literature

Sylvia Bowman, Indiana University

GENERAL EDITOR

SPAIN

Gerald Wade, Vanderbilt University

EDITOR

Juan Meléndez Valdés

(TWAS 302)

TWAYNE'S WORLD AUTHORS SERIES (TWAS)

The purpose of TWAS is to survey the major writers —novelists, dramatists, historians, poets, philosophers, and critics—of the nations of the world. Among the national literatures covered are those of Australia, Canada, China, Eastern Europe, France, Germany, Greece, India, Italy, Japan, Latin America, the Netherlands, New Zealand, Poland, Russia, Scandinavia, Spain, and the African nations, as well as Hebrew, Yiddish, and Latin Classical literatures. This survey is complemented by Twayne's United States Authors Series and English Authors Series.

The intent of each volume in these series is to present a critical-analytical study of the works of the writer; to include biographical and historical material that may be necessary for understanding, appreciation, and critical appraisal of the writer; and to present all material in clear, concise English—but not to vitiate the scholarly content of the work by doing so.

Juan Meléndez Valdés

By R. MERRITT COX
College of William and Mary

Twayne Publishers, Inc. :: New York

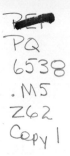

Library of Congress Cataloging in Publication Data

Cox, Ralph Merritt, 1939–
    Juan Meléndez Valdés.

    (Twayne's world authors series, TWAS 302. Spain)
    Bibliography: p.
    1. Meléndez Valdés, Juan, 1754–1817.
PQ6538.M5Z62   861'.4   73–15583
ISBN 0–8057–2918–6

MANUFACTURED IN THE UNITED STATES OF AMERICA

For Grabow

Preface

This book on Juan Meléndez Valdés is a general study of his life and work. Its five chapters comprise five closely knit subjects. The first chapter is a sketch of the poet's life with pertinent facts provided for a basic comprehension of his attitudes. The second is a study of his poetry in relation to artistic trends, particularly of the first half of the eighteenth century. The third traces the development of the more philosophical aspects of his poems from their early, heavy endowment with Locke's sensationalist philosophy to the poet's own quite personal, Romantic one. The fourth chapter is an analysis of the humanitarian sentiments Meléndez expresses in his poetry and the resultant political stances he took in the chaotic period from the French Revolution until his death in 1817. The last chapter is an analysis of Meléndez' *Discursos forenses* (*Legal Discourses*) published in 1821. These prose essays provide an excellent study of the inherently humanitarian aspect of Meléndez' Romanticism.

The Chronology comes essentially from William Colford's and Georges Demerson's studies of Meléndez, with some data added from Quintana and other early biographers. The bibliography at the end is selective, with only the most important items for Meléndez and his times.

I discovered early that the enormous amount of poetry Meléndez produced caused extreme difficulty in its analysis. Because of the great quantity, I chose to follow the three general viewpoints of Chapters Two, Three, and Four. The variety of Meléndez' poetic themes is easily seen in these chapters. Rather than devote a separate chapter to his poetics, I have discussed the meter, form, musicality, tone, etc., of some poems at different places in the book. Most of the quotations are in English, the translations being my own. I have included the original Spanish of some poems, however, in order to emphasize certain points I have made and also to permit the reader of Spanish a further awareness of Meléndez' style.

The reader will note also that I have not always supplied dates for the poems mentioned or discussed in the book. I discovered that some commentators have tended to study Meléndez' poetry chronologically, thinking they observe a youthful frivolity in some of his writings in contrast to what they consider a more mature attitude in later works. I do not feel that this approach is desirable, and thus, to understand Meléndez' poetry better in its totality, I have deliberately omitted dates unless these are important for reasons that will become clear.

Finally, I hope that this book will give the reader a complete picture of what and how the poet wrote and will provide him with an understanding of Meléndez Valdés as a very gifted, versatile artist and a very humane, enlightened man.

R. MERRITT COX

Williamsburg

Contents

Chronology

1754   March 11: Juan Meléndez Valdés is born on this day in the town of Ribera del Fresno (Extremadura) to Juan Antonio Meléndez Romero Compañón y Guijarro and María Cacho Montero de la Vanda.

1761   June 21: Meléndez' mother dies.

1767–   Meléndez goes to school in Madrid at the *Convento de*
1770   *Santo Tomás.*

1770–   He is in school at the *Reales Estudios de San Isidro* in
1772   Madrid.

1772   Meléndez enters the University of Salamanca.

1773   His friendship with José Cadalso begins.

1774   August 13: Meléndez' father dies.

1775   August 23: Meléndez receives his *Bachillerato.*

1776   The friendship between Meléndez and Jovellanos begins and initiates a voluminous correspondence over the years. Meléndez also suffers a serious illness in this year.

1777   June 4: Meléndez' brother Esteban dies.

1778   October 26: Meléndez is chosen as *sustituto* for the Chair in Humanities at Salamanca.

1780   Meléndez is awarded first prize by the Royal Academy of the Language for his eclogue "Batilo."

1781   The poet finally meets his mentor Jovellanos face to face in Madrid. He presents his ode *A la gloria de las artes* before the Academy of St. Ferdinand and is appointed Professor of Classical Languages at the University of Salamanca.

1782   September 28: Meléndez is awarded the *Licenciatura* at the University.

1782   November 22: He is married to María Andrea de Coca.

1783   March 11: He receives his Doctor of Laws degree.

1784   His pastoral play *Las bodas de Camacho el rico* (*The Wedding of the Wealthy Camacho*) wins first prize in a competition sponsored by the city of Madrid celebrating the peace treaty with England and the birth of twin heirs to the Spanish throne.

1785 Meléndez' first volume of poetry is published to immediate and wide acclaim.

1789 May 22: Meléndez is notified of his nomination as magistrate in the Criminal Court at Zaragoza.

1791 In the spring of this year he is promoted to a judgeship and transferred to Valladolid.

1792 He is sent by the government to oversee the unification of five small hospitals in Ávila.

1797 Meléndez is appointed District Attorney of Madrid. A three-volume edition of his works is published, and Goya paints his portrait in the latter part of this year.

1798 Meléndez is elected to the Royal Academy. Because of politics he is also relieved of his duties as District Attorney and ordered to Medina del Campo.

1800 December 3: Meléndez is now fully retired from his office as District Attorney and is ordered to Zamora.

1802 June 27: His salary as District Attorney is restored and the restriction on his place of residence is at last lifted.

1802– During these relatively peaceful years for the poet-jurist
1808 he stays in Salamanca.

1808 He returns to Madrid in the spring and is sent to Asturias by the *Junta Central* to report back on recent public disorders there. He is nearly killed by a mob.

1813 Meléndez goes into exile in France with the fall of the Bonaparte government in Spain.

1815 The prologue to the 1820 edition of his poetry is written in Nîmes.

1817 May 24: Meléndez dies in Montpellier.

1820 The four-volume edition of his poetry containing the biographical essay by Quintana is published.

1821 Meléndez' *Discursos forenses (Legal Discourses)* are published.

CHAPTER 1

Life of Juan Meléndez Valdés

I *Meléndez in His Earliest Years*

MELÉNDEZ returned [1781] to Salamanca which to his misfortune he left some years later [1789] for a career as a magistrate. This departure was the cause of all his future difficulties. It was the reason too that this man—so gentle, childlike, and submissive—had such a hard, stormy existence like that of an extremely ambitious adventurer. There were to be exiles, imprisonments, a near execution as a traitor to his country, and his death in France when he was totally disillusioned, old, and poor. All this for Meléndez—who had never asked for more than a tranquil spot to write his verses!"[1] This quotation from Emilio Cotarelo y Mori in the late nineteenth century is a succinct comment on Juan Meléndez Valdés. For various reasons, particularly for its ironic implications, it serves very nicely as an introduction to the present study of the poet. Meléndez was indeed a gentle man, but not quite the weakling Cotarelo portrays above. Other critics, at more length, have also described him in similarly slighting ways. It is hoped that from the following pages the reader will see that Meléndez Valdés was a strong person and a versatile poet, not a coward or simply a writer of pretty, vapid verses.

Juan Meléndez Valdés was born on March 11, 1754, in Ribera del Fresno in Extremadura and was baptized on March 24 with the name of Juan Antonio Esteban Eulogio. He was the son of Juan Antonio Meléndez Romero Compañón y Guijarro and María Cacho Montero de la Vanda. They were already somewhat advanced in age to be having children, forty-six and forty years old respectively, at their son's birth. They had been married some twenty-one years and already had had several other children.[2] Only two of these children, Esteban Antonio and Agustina Isabel Antonia Serafina, and the poet himself lived to be adults. The family was relatively well situated financially, but not necessarily of a wealthy or noble background. The father, Juan Antonio, possessed several houses in Ribera, but these were quite humble dwellings. His position in the village was hardly more outstanding than the appearance of these houses would indicate—he was steward to a lay brotherhood, the Confraternity of Our Lady of Carmen.

In 1757 the family moved to the neighboring town of Almendralejo. It was here that the young Meléndez probably began his first studies under the tutelage of his father and the care of a servant, Evarista.[3] Lessons in Spanish and Latin were his principal schooling at this point.

Meléndez' mother died in Almendralejo in 1761, and his father nearly died there in 1763. When Meléndez left to continue his studies in Madrid in 1767, his father returned to Ribera to be near his daughter, Agustina, now married to a doctor there.[4] An early nineteenth-century source gives us a good picture of what occurred to Meléndez at this time:

When he had finished his first studies, Meléndez was sent to Madrid to study philosophy under the Dominicans of St. Thomas, his father putting him in the care of an uncle [. . .] named Valdés. [It was from him that Meléndez took the name of Valdés.] The latter, when he saw the studiousness, talent, and pleasant character of his nephew, came to love him with extreme tenderness. These same qualities also attracted his teachers who, as more immediate observers of his abilities, became quickly acquainted with his advances and greatly applauded a poetic composition he wrote for the festivities on the Day of St. Thomas of Aquinas. This poem, like others he was already writing with great fervor, foretold the road he would gloriously follow to the peak of the Spanish Parnassus.[5]

Manuel José Quintana is hardly less glowing in his published account of Meléndez. Describing the atmosphere of these years in Madrid, he writes of Meléndez: "Already at this early time his peaceful, docile nature caused all who knew him to love him. Because of his studiousness and rapid advances as a student, he quickly gained the admiration of his teachers and fellow students. It was at this time that his fondness for poetry began, although his talent and good taste were not quite of the same quality as his fondness. The Restorer of the Spanish Parnassus wrote ballads imitating Gerardo Lobo and composed verses to St. Thomas of Aquinas to please his teachers." [6]

In 1770 Meléndez entered the *Reales Estudios de San Isidro* in Madrid, where he remained for two years studying Greek and philosophy. In the years he was in the capital he was not entirely away from his family. His older brother Esteban was there as secretary to Alonso de Llanes, future Bishop of Segovia and Archbishop of Seville. The relationship with his brother was very close, Esteban serving as a sort of father *in absentia*. The connection with the Bishop was to prove fruitful as well, for it was he who pressed him to enter the University of Salamanca in 1772. After this date Meléndez continued to spend his summers in Madrid with his brother. With the death of their father in 1774, Meléndez drew even closer to Esteban, who toward the end of that same year moved with his superior to Segovia where Llanes began his duties as the new Bishop.

The year 1774 was an important one in Meléndez' life. The death of his father was a tremendous blow to him and left him, a still impressionable, sensitive youth, an orphan at the age of twenty. The loss of both parents combined with the relatively early separation from his family in 1767 left a profound mark on Meléndez' outlook on life and undoubtedly is one basic reason for the escapism noted in his early poetry. The death of his father pushed him even closer to his brother and provided the poet with a certain stability that he would otherwise have totally lacked. The increased attendance in the Bishop's house at Segovia also allowed him to meet influential people who would be valuable to him in the coming years.

II *Meléndez as a Student at Salamanca*

At the ancient University in Salamanca Meléndez continued his study of the Classics begun in Madrid, but he also took up judicial studies. The combination might at first appear ambivalent, even paradoxical, but this double field of interest would form the essential core of his life from this time on. In his first year at Salamanca he was busy studying principally Justinian and the *Institutions* of Antonio Torres, a professor there. His work in Greek was under the guidance of a Father Zamora. He became increasingly aware that his interests needed amplification in the fields of history, philosophy, and *belles-lettres*. In 1778 he wrote to Gaspar Melchor de Jovellanos about his first years in the University:

In the first year of my studies, without a guide or anyone who might direct me, I read the *Moral Philosophy and Natural Law* of Heineccius [German jurist, 1681–1741 . . .] and another work of Heineccius, the *History of Civil Law.* This was in the summer, and in the following year, after finishing these studies, with Cadalso I went over the *Law of Man* by Vattel, [Swiss jurist, 1714–1767], and a good part of the *Spirit of Laws* [Montesquieu. . . .] And thus I continued instructing myself never leaving Heineccius totally aside. If this great man had only left some elements of a law code, we would have had from him the most complete system of law [. . . .] His dissertations and essays are a treasure of erudition of the purest Latin. Finally, he is such that he has me completely bewitched and, reading him, I shall miss nothing. His excellent method helps a great deal, for I like methodical authors who search out the real reasons for things. I do not care for long expositions, exceptions, or particular cases. I want to be given the principal reasons with good, solid foundations. I myself will reach my own conclusions.[7]

Meléndez' clear thinking, his serious nature especially concerning the interpretation of law, and a certain self-assertiveness all stand out very prominently in this letter written at an early age.

One of the most important friends Meléndez made outside his family is mentioned in this same letter. José Cadalso was the one who initially urged him to study Vattel and Montesquieu. Stationed at Salamanca during Meléndez' second year as a student, the young military officer became an intimate confidant and mentor. Cadalso provided a sophistication and polish that naturally attracted Meléndez at this impressionable period in his life. Not quite twenty when he met Cadalso, he began to see other worlds than the purely Spanish, provincial one he had been inhabiting. Cadalso was only thirty-three years old, widely traveled, and above all a soldier and poet. Given the inherently romantic inclinations of Meléndez, he could only have been attracted by Cadalso's attitudes.

Cadalso's knowledge of languages was excellent. This was not an unimportant asset as he was to direct Meléndez particularly in his choice of reading and study and in the earliest directions of his writing. Cadalso was already recognized as a man of letters, having written in various genres. A tragedy

entitled *Don Sancho García* had appeared in 1771. A biting prose
satire, much in the vogue of the period and probably influential
in the early career of Tomás de Iriarte, was finished in 1772
and called *Los eruditos a la violeta* (*The Pseudo-Intellectuals*).
Most recently he had published a collection of poetry entitled
Ocios de mi juventud (*Pastimes of My Youth*).

Cadalso's greatest contribution to Meléndez' development,
aside from a purely stylistic one, was a psychological and moral
one. It was he who really opened the younger man's eyes to life
and helped him form a *modus vivendi*. Cadalso was a gentleman
and a patriot, but these attributes did not prevent his expressing
a certain cynicism about the world around him. However, cynicism is usually only the outer covering of the true idealist, and
because of his more profound idealism, candor, and sensitivity,
Cadalso was first able to approach Meléndez. Indeed, it was the
seeming paradox of idealism and cynicism that enabled him to
influence Meléndez all the more. In a letter Cadalso wrote to
Tomás de Iriarte sometime during this period we can see his
intriguing, teasing personality asserting itself:

What difference can it make to you [Iriarte] whether I have arrived in
Salamanca or whether I have died on the road, whether I am well or
not, happy or sad, unattached or in love, bored or entertained, in a
good inn or in a hospital? Well, to me it matters a great deal that you
know I admire you very much and therefore send you notice of having
arrived here well, of being in a good humor, well ensconced with my
books, and rather favored by the people of Salamanca. This very
learned University is where they do not teach mathematics, physics,
anatomy, natural history, common law, oriental languages, or any
other such foolish thing. Rather it produces people who with resound-
ing voices declaim their 77, 777 syllogisms on how the angels talk in
their *tertulias*, on whether the heavens are made of the metal of bells
or liquids like the lightest wine, or stupid similar things that both you
and I know we shall never know, learn, or study.[8]

It is Meléndez himself who best summed up what Cadalso
was to him when he wrote to a friend after Cadalso's death.
We find neatly expressed all the ways—psychological, intellectual,
emotional—in which the older man had helped him. The adulation
of this letter, written from Salamanca on March 16, 1782, is by no
means false or empty. Cadalso had been killed in battle at Gibral-

tar the night of February 27, 1782. Meléndez is not quite thirty years old and still vividly remembers the first emotional impact made on him by Cadalso some ten years before. He writes to Salvador de Mena:

My dear Mena: How have you received the news of our unfortunate Cadalso? You did not know him, but a man like him is a common loss for all sensitive souls. My own soul curses war a thousand times, this war that has deprived me of such a good friend to whom I shall be all my life indebted for his most intimate recognition. *Without him, I would be nothing today* [italics mine]. My tastes, my fondness for good books, my poetic talents, my literature such as it is—all are due to him. He approached me in the second year of my studies; he opened my eyes; he taught me; he inspired in me this noble enthusiasm for friendship and for good; he formed my sense of judgment. He performed with me all the duties of a loving father with his most beloved son.[9]

The one other significant influence on Meléndez' literary and philosophical development at about the same time as Cadalso's came from Gaspar Melchor de Jovellanos. The relationship between the two began in 1776 when Father Diego González, friend and mentor also of Meléndez, wrote Jovellanos about the young poet. A correspondence went on between Jovellanos and Meléndez for five years before they finally met each other face to face in Madrid in 1781. Jovellanos' relationship with Meléndez at first was much like Cadalso's, but it soon lost some of its moralistic, paternalistic tone to take on a more intellectual one.

In the academic year of 1774–1775, Meléndez continued the plan of studies he had begun in 1772. He diligently worked at his law courses, but he also studied Greek and Latin. His writing of poetry was not neglected, and by the end of this year Meléndez thought himself ready to take the examination for the *Bachillerato*. He studied prodigiously all the summer of 1775 and at its end received the degree.

Not long after, Meléndez began work on his *Licenciatura*. He was no longer just a student of the Classics because during the new academic year he was promoted to the position of professor: for two months he was a substitute professor of Greek.[10] At this time he taught himself English, and by the end of the year he was able to read the language and understand it fairly well when spoken.

Because of all his activities, however, his health deteriorated. One wonders just how much the death of his father in 1774 influenced the development of his illness. After his father died, the poet truly began to push ahead in his work, perhaps in part to stifle the isolation he must have felt. The new friendship with Cadalso undoubtedly helped him, as we have seen, but it may unconsciously also have pressed him even more to move into new fields and directions. Given Meléndez' sensitive and at times frenetic personality, he must have been influenced to a tremendous degree by these external occurrences.

The result finally was a physical breakdown. During most of the year 1776 Meléndez suffered from a fever, chest pains, and headaches which often went on for days. A total collapse took place in the autumn because he refused to take proper care of himself. His breakdown seems almost self-willed. Father Diego González sought to impose some sort of order and sense in the youth's life, but usually met with little success. He tried to get him into the country for long rests, forcing Meléndez to be a sort of *beatus ille*. One of Meléndez' lady friends, the Ciparis of his poetry, invited him to spend several months at her family's home in the country. The enforced relaxation finally worked and Meléndez by the end of 1776 had begun his way back to full health and was able to return to the University in January, 1777.

The ensuing months were not to be very pleasant, however, for in April Meléndez' brother, Esteban, his last close tie to his family, became seriously ill. The letters that Meléndez wrote to Jovellanos during the months of April, May, and June reveal his mental and emotional state at the time. They are of interest because they show us exactly what Meléndez was like in his innermost personality. They help as well in defining the role of Jovellanos in the poet's life. We have already seen that a correspondence between the two had begun in 1776. The first letter we cite here is dated from Salamanca on April 14, 1777, and reads in part:

When I was hoping to write you at length, I find myself again unable to do not only that but even to write at all, my head bewildered by a jumble of sad thoughts and my heart full of affliction. I have just received the unhappy news that my brother in Segovia is quite ill. He is the only one who remains to me. It was he who guided me, and to him I owe the first seeds of virtue. My parents being dead now, I have only him in their place, and only he is able in some way to fill their absence. What a piece of news for me! What a state I shall be in! I leave here in the morning to fulfill my duties and to attend him— or to die from grief at his side.[11]

In May from Segovia Meléndez wrote to Jovellanos: "I appreciate your fine expression of affection and your great interests in my feelings [. . . .] My brother is about the same [. . . .] I think that in the end nothing will be improved because the doctors believe he is tubercular [. . . .]"[12]

In a letter dated June 8, Meléndez gives full expression to his emotions, precipitated by the death of his brother. His vulnerability, his feeling of isolation, and his need for a guiding hand all stand out here in vivid detail. He turns to Jovellanos much as a lost child to its father. The tone of their relationship, which becomes more intimate from this time on, is succinctly stated at the end of the letter. The role of Jovellanos in Meléndez' life is thus very early established. Meléndez writes:

My dear Jovino: When I had hoped to tell you the pleasant news of the recovery of my brother, I must write you the painful news of his death the fourth of this month [. . .] leaving me in the most complete solitude and abandonment, which you can easily imagine. He had been almost without a fever for several days and then, when everyone was counting on his recovery, a new attack suddenly occurred which within five days killed him. Since then my eyes have not been dry, and neither can I find anything nor can anyone tell me anything that will give me the presence of mind which the situation of the moment calls for [. . . .] The image of my brother is always with me. How much worry! How much anxiety! And how much attendance on him—all to no avail! Nothing, nothing was able to save him. Oh, my Jovino! I wish you were here at my side to temper my pain and tears with your counsel and, embracing me, share my sorrow, oh, my faithful friend.[13]

By August Meléndez had regained his control. He writes to Jovellanos from Salamanca on the second of the month clearly stating how Jovellanos will henceforth be his guide. The desire for a guide, a staying hand, is intriguing in Meléndez. He is twenty-three years old and seemingly should be able to set his own path. One wonders again about the emotional significance of the loss of his father in 1774. Perhaps, too, the poet's feeling of isolation goes back further to the death of his mother when he was still a child. In the following letter he feels terribly alone and looks to Jovellanos to be his guide, to replace the family he has lost:

My very dear friend: The very sound advice you gave me in regard to the excess of my emotion has left me a little confused and much encouraged. I cannot deny, nevertheless, that when I read your letter I cried infinite tears and I was almost unable to sleep the entire night. But these tears were more from friendship and affection for you than from sentiment itself on seeing my lack of merit, my youth, my lack of protection, and all those other things I find every time I look at myself, more worthy of pity and contempt than esteem [. . . .] I shall never be anything nor worth anything nor shall I be able to distinguish myself in anything. Yet if Fortune should make something of all this, I shall confess I owe it to you because from this day forth you will be my brother who will direct and advise me [. . . .] I for my part promise you never to become unworthy, with all that is in my power, of this new title of your friend.[14]

Meléndez returned to Salamanca in the late summer and began his work at the University much as if nothing had happened; that is, on the surface he continued as before. The same intensity that had driven him earlier pushed him now. William Colford believes that part of the reason for his renewed vigor was due to the Bishop of Segovia, his brother's employer.[15] The Bishop, who had helped him for the last five years, was urging him to enter the church, to escape the pleasures of the world which he feared Meléndez enjoyed too much. Meléndez was contemplating taking holy orders, but was unable to make up his mind satisfactorily. In the last letter quoted above, he also speaks to Jovellanos about his relations with the Bishop:

The Bishop of Segovia, whom my brother served as secretary, has put me under his protection and has honored me a great deal with his favors. The goodness of his heart and his kind actions and close friendship with my brother from the time of his deputation in the capital cause me to have complete confidence in his beneficence. Nevertheless, you can do me a favor by writing to him and recommending me. This will put me in even higher standing with him because he will see that, even though I am very young, you honor me with your friendship and that I myself try to have such distinguished friends. I believe that when I finish my course, which will be next year or the beginning of the following, he will perhaps want to give me some position near him, according to what his confessor has given me to understand. I could find nothing more pleasing than this although my inclination toward the priesthood is not the greatest. But an upright man, if he does not find any open resistance must sacrifice everything, even his own inclinations, to the desire and service of his benefactor. There is still plenty of time, and if the situation should arise, I shall do nothing without your advice and opinion.[16]

Meléndez was not to be so tolerant when the "situation" did arise. When the Bishop remonstrated with him in the early fall about his worldly vanity, Meléndez was hardly so agreeable as his August letter indicates he would be. He reacts quite violently in a letter written to Jovellanos from Salamanca in October. I find the tone of both the August and the October letters most revealing of Meléndez' basic personality. The young man is hardly that emotional weakling at times alluded to by some of his biographers and critics. Neither does he express the insecurity we saw a few days after his brother's death. Meléndez, like most sensitive people, could go to extremes in his emotional reactions. He could call to others for help, especially those in power or who showed much sense of worldly direction. Certainly the Bishop was not without influence, and up to this time Meléndez had been quite willing to accept his attention. Yet it is to Jovellanos that Meléndez turns now for any real help. The reason for his doing so was not simply a refusal to closet himself in the confines of the Church. The basic reason was his own acute sense of judgment. He was by no means an impractical man, but one who had a great deal of common sense. Speaking of the contents of the following letter from a psychological point of view, we must understand that Meléndez consciously realized what was the better choice for him—the world with its public acclaim, the world that Jovellanos more than anyone else at this time could help him enter. If we are to understand certain events in Meléndez' later life, particularly his entrance into the judicial world, we have to realize what he is doing now. The writer's firmness, his indignation, and his inherent spirit of rebellion are all blatantly evident in the letter below. They manifest themselves naturally and openly from this time on. His words to Jovellanos are thus very revealing:

My very dear friend [. . .] Who would believe that my lord [the Bishop] could suspect in me the slightest sign of vanity or that he would impute to me a defect so opposite to my character and my situation? I hardly slept last night because of this thought and I do not know what to attribute it to or indeed what to think at all. Fantasy presents me with a thousand things but none satisfies me. And then, when I look myself over well, I find myself so far from being vain as the sky is from the earth and that, rather, my humility becomes almost embarrassing. In short, my friend, if my verses and my letters cannot tell you what my character is really like, while I still have not had the pleasure of seeing you, this asseveration of mine at least must prevent you from judging also in the same way.[17]

Because of the wound he felt at the hands of the Bishop, whether rightly or wrongly, and because of his continued interest in his work at the University, he now definitely turned toward teaching as his future career. He was named a substitute for Dr. Manuel Blengua, and for a month was responsible for teaching Civil Institutions.[18] His studies were carried on at a rapid pace. In addition, he began to do some tutoring. His comments to Jovellanos in a letter from Salamanca dated January 16, 1778, are indicative of his developing outlook: "I cannot devote myself to long compositions that demand much study and meditation. The duties of my teaching, Law, and the care of my pupil keep me busy night and day. I cannot emphasize too much how I like this last duty and how much it has made me think and read about the question of education. I want to give him the best education possible and do right in every way and this causes me to be neither satisfied nor content with whatever I do. But I shall speak to you more at length about all this on another occasion [. . . .]"[19] During the summer of 1778 he began to prepare assiduously for his examination for the *Licenciatura*, hoping to finish this requirement the next year. However, it was to be actually three more years before he would take the examination.

On October 26, 1778, the University chose Meléndez to occupy the Chair of Humanities as a *sustituto*. His duty was very much to his liking as it involved the presentation of the works of Horace. Even though he had achieved a rather remarkable post for one so young and with only a *Bachillerato,* he was not satisfied. For the next three years he was to make repeated efforts to get a full-time position in either Law or Humanities. In October, 1778, he applied for the Chair in Civil Institutions. In 1780 he made two other attempts to obtain a position in Law. Demerson has discovered even a third post he sought in that same year. On October 19, 1779, his apprenticeship as a jurist was approved also.[20]

The years 1780 and 1781 witnessed the beginning of Meléndez' public literary success. Several years before, the Royal Academy of the Language had established literary competitions awarding prizes for compositions in prose and poetry that best treated a designated subject. These contests, not always important because of the works produced for them but more because they celebrated events of national glory and renown, awakened an interest in Spain's past. In the first competition which ran from late September, 1777, to midsummer, 1778, the subject for prose was a eulogy of Philip V, the idea being to praise the king responsible for the founding of the Royal Academy. The winner was José de Viera y Clavijo, perhaps most remembered today for his biographical, historical study of the Canary Islands. The prize was not awarded, however, until June 22, 1779, because the subject proved too arduous to complete satisfactorily in the time allotted.[21] The theme for poetry concerned Cortez' destruction of his ships at the beginning of his conquest of Mexico. This theme was felt to be most heroic, and we sense behind it an attempt to produce a national epic on the order of the *Aeneid* or *Os Lusiadas.* Interestingly, in 1779 the *Poem of the Cid* would be published for the first time by Tomás Antonio Sánchez. Forty-five compositions were presented in the poetry division of the competition. The prize went to an unknown poet, José María Vaca de Guzmán y Derechos, on August 13, 1778.

The theme for poetry in the contest of 1779–1780 was a praise of country life to be written in an eclogue of five hundred to six hundred lines. Meléndez submitted a poem entitled "Batilo. Égloga en alabanza de la vida del campo" ("Batilo. Eclogue in Praise of Country Life"). He received first prize which was awarded on Mach 18, 1780. Tomás de Iriarte won second prize for his eclogue called "La felicidad de la vida del campo" ("The Happiness of Country Life"). Both works were published under the auspices of the Academy. This competition involved Meléndez in the first really public polemic of his literary career. Juan Pablo Forner stepped in and defended him, not selflessly, however, one hastens to add, and so prevented Meléndez from having to carry on one of those endless, public debates so popular in this century.[22]

On December 9, 1780, a piece of news was spread about that was to prove very important in Meléndez' life. A notice was posted in Salamanca that, because of the death of the head of the Department of Classical Languages, the Chair of that department would be filled by a competitive examination. The candidates would have a half hour to explain a passage chosen at random from Homer, an hour commenting on an ode of Horace, and one final hour to discuss either Greek or Latin grammar, literature, and institutions. Meléndez took the examination on January 19, 1781, along with eight other candidates. His passage from Homer was verses one through four of Book III of the *Iliad*; his ode from Horace was number ten of Book II: *Rectius vives, Licini, neque altum*; and the third part concerned his preparation in Latin.[23] The examinations and *curricula* were sent to Madrid so that the King, Charles III, himself, might publicly designate the new appointee. This enlightened monarch's participation in educational reforms is very forcefully seen in this action. On August 9, 1781, Meléndez was announced as the new professor.

In July, Meléndez had gone to Madrid to meet his mentor Jovellanos. It does seem a bit strange that after five years of correspondence he finally gets around to seeing the person who had become, according to the young poet's own words, his father, brother, and idol all wrapped in one. Meléndez no doubt did very much want to see this man who had helped him so much and whom he loved and admired tremendously. He must also have had the quite sagacious intention of pushing his candidacy for the Chair at Salamanca. Jovellanos, a justice in the *Sala de Alcaldes de Casa y Corte*, with his contacts at court could help him all the more forcefully if Meléndez was there for important introductions. Whether this lobbying was really in Meléndez' mind or not when he went to Madrid, within a few weeks he had the post which he so greatly coveted.

While Meléndez was in Madrid staying in Jovellanos' home

in this summer of 1781, a new occasion arose for him to show his talents. This was the triennial distribution of prizes in painting, sculpture, and architecture by the Royal Academy of St. Ferdinand. As if various currents in his life were converging at one point and at the same time, Meléndez was experiencing a climax of glory and renown toward which all his youthful years had been leading him. As in other instances, it was again the influence of friends that was helping him in part. Jovellanos was to make a speech at the meeting of the Academy, and he invited Meléndez to compose an ode on the occasion. Even though we emphasized Meléndez' political maneuverings in seeking the University appointment while in Madrid, it is very probable that initially he went to Madrid to present his ode at the Academy celebration. He arrived early in July, as we noted above, and the festivities were to take place on the fourteenth of the month. As Colford points out, if the invitation to compose the poem, necessarily appropriate for the occasion, had been extended after Meléndez' arrival in the capital, it is hard to see how he could have produced the monumental ode that he did, called "A la gloria de las artes" ("To the Glory of the Arts").[24] The audience was highly impressed with the perfection of his work. It was later published at the expense of the Royal Academy of St. Ferdinand, and Meléndez himself was made an honorary member of the Academy. This particular honor, coming on the heels of his triumph in 1780 at the Royal Academy of the Language, catapulted the young poet into the public spotlight and caused his reputation to spread very rapidly.

Even though Meléndez' new appointment at the University of Salamanca took effect on August 9, he stayed on longer in the capital. He undoubtedly enjoyed the accolades that poured in. Probably at this time he also posed for a bust of himself which was to go in the Academy of St. Ferdinand. He was formally inducted into the University faculty by proxy on August 22 and took up his new duties soon afterward. Meléndez still had only his *Bachillerato*. His eager intentions a year or two earlier of taking the examination for the *Licenciatura* had obviously been postponed. He had been so busy teaching, composing his poems, and preparing for the examinations for the new professorship that he had been unable to prepare himself adequately for the examinations for his next degree. He now set himself to this task with renewed vigor. There must surely have been, too, the haunting realization in his mind that he had no really advanced degree. He probably was not without some feeling of insecurity about the written proof of his capabilities. That he had proved himself capable on the examinations for the position could not completely allay this preoccupation. At the close of that academic year he came up before a twelve-man board which unanimously awarded him the degree on September 28, 1782. Less than six months later, on March 11, 1783, his twenty-ninth birthday, he received the degree of Doctor of Laws. Meléndez could now proudly hold his new Chair. His brilliant and inspired ten years of study at Salamanca had culminated quite satisfactorily.

III   *Marriage of Meléndez and Years of Teaching*

Even though much of Meléndez' poetry treats his love for young ladies, there are few really concrete references to the relations he had with them. A note in Mesonero Romanos' *Memorias de un setentón* (*Memories of an Old Gentleman*), charming in itself, indicates the tantalizing, elusive quality of these references. It provides implications rather than facts. Mesonero relates how when he was a boy, an old lady was once greatly affected by his recitation of some poetry: "In 1816 one night while Doña Rosa de la Nueva y Tapia was at the home of my parents [. . .] I [. . .] had just recited some compositions of the celebrated Salmantine poets. I found among the poems the beautiful ballad by Meléndez entitled "Rosana en los fuegos" ("Rosana in Love"). Hardly had I finished reciting it when doña Rosa with tears in her eyes and smothering me with kisses and embraces took out a small portrait [. . . .] 'Take it, my son,' she said. 'This portrait was engraved in Paris more than thirty years ago. It is the portrait of the Rosana of Meléndez, the very same one who gives it to you now so that you will keep it in memory of her and of her tender poet.' " 25

When Meléndez married, however, it was to a woman rather different from the somewhat ephemeral ones portrayed in his poetry: "[In 1782] he had married doña María Andrea de Coca y Figueroa, a native of Salamanca and daughter of one of the most distinguished families of that city. But since his new Chair gave him really little to do and since he had no children from his marriage, the poet [. . .] remained free to follow his favorite pursuits and to devote himself entirely to philosophy and letters." [26] Quintana's rather amusingly understated announcement of Meléndez' marriage has much the same surprising effect on the reader today as Meléndez' own announcement had on his friends. The marriage ceremony was performed with great secrecy, and for this reason has caused critics to assert both 1782 and 1783 as the year it took place. Demerson, as with so many previously cloudy facts in Meléndez' life, has established the date as November 22, 1782.[27] All manner of precautions were taken to prevent news of the event leaking out. The witnesses were either members of the bride's family or close friends of Meléndez. The official announcement was made on February 6, 1783, that "Félix Martín Básquez, priest of the parish of San Benito, having been made aware of the act of marriage effected by Mathías [the bride's father . . .] gives his nuptial benediction to the newlyweds solemnizing the marriage in the church in the presence of Domingo García, Joseph de Coca, Ignacio de la Riva, and others [. . . .]" [28]

The reasons for the secrecy of the marriage are still obscure, even after Demerson's discoveries. The marriage was canonically legal, but for some reason was felt best left socially unannounced at first. There have been many conjectures as to why the couple wanted this secrecy. Most critics, following veiled comments by Quintana and quite venomous attacks by José Somoza in the nineteenth century, have tended to lay the blame on the wife. I include a lengthy quotation from Somoza first published in 1843 and later in Volume 61 of the *Biblioteca de Autores Españoles* (to be abbreviated as *BAE* henceforth). The writer appears rather bitter against the woman whom Meléndez married. His words are as revealing about his own hang-ups as they are about the marriage itself:

I had come to have a great fear and aversion for marriage because I remembered so vividly that of my teacher Meléndez. He was tied to one of those women who cannot be judged bad publicly but who nevertheless are intolerable. And here is another digression about this singular woman who dominated that famous writer and caused his errors and misfortunes. María Andrea de Coca was of the noble Salamancan family Maldonado. She had a certain beauty, and she even would have had charm if she had been endowed with a better character. Women with bad temper need to be doubly beautiful so as not to seem monsters. The day when Meléndez asked advice about this marriage of the happy Iglesias, of the energetic Cienfuegos, and of other friends of his, there was not a single one who approved of it. Each one gave a description of the future bride in a different style, each less favorable than the other. But Meléndez shut them all up when he confessed that he was already secretly married. Indeed, it was a rather extravagant match between the gentle Meléndez and that crazy woman. The Devil incarnate, her own father called her. Please believe me, my young readers! What there is of virtue in her sex one cannot fault her in the least. But what virtue, my Lord!—haughty, unapproachable, hostile—like that of some of the heroines of Calderón or Moreto, both of whom she was extremely fond. It is probable that no single mortal ever dared offer her a flattering remark, for if he had he would never have escaped an almost certain slap in the face. Her talents and learning were perverted by an extravagant sense of judgment. Her passions were so extreme that they made some of her good qualities seem vices: trying to be economical, she became niggardly and instead of being honestly ambitious she seemed covetous. Instead of the simple, wifely love she really did feel, she expressed more the feelings of an intolerant fishwife, the implacable executioner of her husband, and the jealous guard against all those who esteemed her husband regardless of their sex. In vain would Meléndez' friends try to talk to him without being disturbed by this devil in human form. It was in vain to try to find a time she would not be around, in vain to climb the stairs on tiptoe to his study. She would say that her *Monsiurito* was hers alone, that his verses were written only for her, that she was the wife of the first man in Spain who really should be Prime Minister. And the funny thing about all this was that the good *Monsiurito* would not contradict her either in words or deeds. But this woman who was the sole cause for Meléndez' weakness and vacillation had a certain goodness of soul that did her honor. In later life whenever contrary opinions were rendered about her ambitious plans, she would say that in a pinch she would set up an oil and vinegar shop so her husband could continue living in a room above, writing for his ungrateful fatherland. Everybody knows that after his death she thought only of the glory of her husband. She succeeded with great difficulty in persuading the government to pay for the edition [1820] of his works. I saw her die on a straw mattress in her servant's house in 1822, still thinking of saving some money to have her husband's remains brought back to Spain, with the idea, of course, of being buried with him and having the epitaph read: "Meléndez and His Wife." [29]

Undoubtedly Somoza's description had some basis in fact, but the underlying tone seems grossly exaggerated. The unfortunate thing about this portrait is the shrewishness ascribed to Meléndez' wife. Biographers and critics in general of Meléndez since the mid-nineteenth century, whether openly quoting Somoza as we have done or not, have been in great part influenced by his sharp criticism of the woman. Some have seen Meléndez' receiving the Doctorate soon after the marriage and his entrance into the judicial life later as results of her influence. Meléndez' wife probably did prod him to leave the teaching profession. However, as implied in the letter to Jovellanos where Meléndez was so angry at the Bishop, he would not have started out in a new direction if he had not been intending to do so because of his own convictions. Meléndez did not act precipitately. His so-called precipitate actions usually had been cooling in his mind for months, sometimes even years. The role of his wife was actually that of a spiritual or, perhaps better said, emotional counselor. Doña María in essence, therefore, took up the role of mother, lover, and wife to Meléndez. Not least of these was the first category. Meléndez' mother had died when he was seven years old. While he never actually wrote openly about his loss, we can sense in that nostalgic, melancholy note of his early poetry the longing desire for a tenderness and even voluptuousness that the child first experiences from his mother. Demerson has unearthed a document that adds more credence to this particular idea. Whereas doña María said her age was "around thirty" when she married, he has discovered that she was born in 1744, making her actually thirty-eight years old in 1782—ten years older than Meléndez.[30]

There are good reasons for considering Meléndez' wife in a positive light. The fact that Meléndez stayed with her the rest of his life is important, for if he had really wanted, he could have left her and taken up with mistresses, a not uncommon practice ever and certainly not in the eighteenth century. Neither are there any statements from him that he did not care for her with great affection and sincerity. It is significant that Somoza does not remember any remark from Meléndez in this regard. Given Somoza's antipathy toward the wife, if he had heard anything negative about her from Meléndez he would certainly have included it in the unflattering commentary quoted above. He

ed by the reactionary ele-
it was not the University's
Spain's backwardness in
rce. Meléndez, in a quite
king and in so doing gained
. His words have again a
from a man who bitterly
any of his contemporaries.
te when he was angry at a
ndez says: "These errors
o not study and progress.
and put ourselves at once
studying—to begin with, the
was not soon resolved, un-
ble outbursts, was not one,
tes as was Forner or Iriarte.
eaving to others the task of

rsity faculty, Meléndez also
amping of the body. It was
niversity was ever to take up
in, it must have outstanding
niversity Chairs henceforth
rit, an indirect attack on the
dez wrote his own ideas on
guing not only for what they
for what they imply of the
time. The examination for a
itten and an oral exam. This
dez would further tighten up
rs to be the holders of Chairs
the examinee. The questions
ty, and—a significant recom-
allow the discussion to go
analyze the subject in great
an oblique reference to the
hin the University at the mo-
put forth as well.37
came involved also in projects
was proposed to establish a

Life of Juan Meléndez Valdés

presents Meléndez as closeted in a cell because of the wife's
police-like care of him. I think that Somoza was deceived, probably because he wanted to be. He refused to understand that
Meléndez preferred to appear retiring, while all along he was
quite subtly making his own way, achieving precisely what he
wanted.

From this marriage Meléndez received certain financial gain.
Until 1789, when he left Salamanca, he lived in the home of his
wife's family. He seems to have gotten along well in this
arrangement, so again we may assume that Meléndez was not
displeased with his marital state.

In the fall of 1783 Meléndez had been at the University of
Salamanca for over ten years and knew well its strong and weak
points. He had by this time been a student and both a part-time
and full-time teacher there. Writing to Eugenio Llaguno y
Amirola in 1782 about his intentions of celebrating the Gibraltar
campaign in an ode or epic poem, he says: "I lack, however, even
the most essential pieces of information because here even a
pawn ticket is considered contraband, and they do not understand anything that is not scholastic or legal questions which
would be just as well off never being treated by us. Studies of
importance are in a horrible abandonment and bad taste sprouts
up and reproduces itself everywhere—a most embarrassing situation for a place that should be an academy of *belles-lettres* and
fruitful knowledge." 31

It is obvious from this stray comment that Meléndez had no
illusions about the place in which he had so ardently sought a
teaching post. As a professor he began, however, to act according
to his rather liberal, enlightened views and became involved in
several public polemics. As we noted earlier, polemics, so much
delighted in by many writers of the time, were not to Meléndez'
tastes. In 1781 he had been quite content to allow Forner to stand
in for him in the verbal duel that Tomás de Iriarte had started
with him over his poem "Batilo." When public debate was
necessary for extrapersonal reasons on the other hand, he was
not at all hesitant to enter the fray. In 1783 he publicly opposed
the rife absenteeism of professors from their classes. He openly
attacked a professor of anatomy, one Francisco Zunzunegui, who
had complained of the impossibility of carrying on his teaching
because of the lack of " 'necessary cadavers for dissection and

the difficulty he had encountered in setting
and a properly equipped room for the st
Meléndez replied "'that the University in e
should oppose the demands of Dr. Zunzune
worked nearly so assiduously as he flattered hi
and that it ask of the official who kept attend
faculty a list of the Doctor's courses [. . . .]'" S
when the subject again arose, Meléndez vig
sanctions against those who repeatedly missed
seemed that the professor of anatomy had not
classes for sixteen months.[32]

In May, 1784, Meléndez became involved in
included the administration of the University and t
government. He appealed to the law faculty again
of the dean to forbid public disputation on six con
he had advanced:

"(1) That punishment is bad which past experience ha:
contrary to the public good. Since a deceitful or erroneou
may increase crime, punishment must be appropriate t
prompt, public, irremissible, and wherever possible, prescr
(2) If the punishment is the same whether the crime i
tended or actually accomplished, being determined merel
cusation, crime is actually encouraged.
(3) The punishment of prisoners is permitted when no oth
seems feasible to preserve orderly rule. But moderation will
what measures are useful and necessary. However, we asse
taliation, mutilation of limbs, and torture are inhuman, sa
injurious.
(4) Guilty persons may rightly be deprived of liberty for a
ited time or have their infamy proclaimed. However, their
may not be violated.
(5) When confiscation is used as a punishment, innocent part
be indirectly injured, and therefore it should not be used exc
very grave crimes.
(6) The punishment that is prescribed by law and intended to :
the crime may have been by chance contrary to the nature
crime; therefore, we wish to warn all to reflect upon the laws n
tablished. Truly, just as mathematicians through study of the sm
part discern the larger whole, so do I bring out from each single
the spirit of [legal] traditions." [33]

[32]

Practice for the University was criticiz
ments in the University who held that
duty to produce statesmen or to stud
agriculture, manufacturing, or comm
forward outburst, denounced such thin
the enmity of many influential peopl
modern sound to them. They come
regretted the insular attitudes of so
He sounds not unlike Tomás de Iriar
particularly backward idea.[35] Melé
[attitudes, i.e.] are the reason we
We must untie ourselves from them
and with great energy to the task of
Spanish language."[36] The question
fortunately. Meléndez, capable of n
however, to carry on prolonged deba
He soon withdrew from the storm,
backbiting and petty feuding.
During these years on the Unive
became involved in a proposed rev
slowly being perceived that if the U
again its force and leadership in Sp
professors. It was decided that
should be given only because of m
existing sycophantic system. Melér
this matter. Some of them are intri
reveal of Meléndez' thinking, but
situation of the University at that
Chair would be composed of a wr
procedure was not new, but Melér
the exam by requiring the examine
closest in subject matter to that o
asked were to be of a great vari
mendation—the examiners were t
where it would without fearing t
detail. This suggestion would see
repressive political atmosphere wi
ment. Other interesting ideas wer
In varying degrees, Meléndez b
outside the University. When it

[34]

branch of the Economic Society *Amigos del País* in Salamanca in 1785, Meléndez, who had been a member of the Basque Society, became interested but took little part in the discussion. He perhaps felt that this worthy proposal, like others he had championed at length, would go the way they had—into the wastebasket. Evidently such was the case, for Demerson finds no trace of the existence of the Society at Salamanca.[38]

Meléndez did actively engage in efforts to set up a printing shop in Salamanca. This project caused a full-scale war inside and outside the faculty. There were more interventions on Meléndez' part just as vituperative as this one and the others noted above.

Whatever the outcomes of these campaigns were, they are important to us for showing basic elements in the poet's personality. A man who would take the politically and intellectually precarious stands that Meléndes did while he was a teacher at Salamanca was certainly not a flighty individual. His actions as well suggest reasoned examination on his part before making his attacks. Reason, however, does not necessarily deny the need for human emotion. Meléndez was an emotional man, extremely sensitive to the plight of his country and his countrymen. His emotional outbursts are those of one who has reached the limits of patience and reacts as only that type of honest, feeling man can. His attitudes are essentially "enlightened," the attitude of a Jovellanos, his mentor, or an Iriarte, or anyone of the acknowledged *ilustrados* of this period. By expressing his viewpoints, even passionately, Meléndez is not unlike these other men who, while praising reason, also let their passions carry them away to a certain extent. Iriarte, for example, manifested this propensity in his polemical treatises. The end result of their involvement was the same for Meléndez as it was for Iriarte in the 1780's—the gaining of mordant enemies. In Meléndez' case, perhaps because he refused to carry on his arguments in written works, we are not always sure of who the various enemies were. Yet in references from this time on we find Meléndez alluding to them, for the most part the blind, reactionary traditionalists that Iriarte also fought. It is ironic that these two men who on the surface had little in common and who publicly were antagonists in the early 1780's should have felt much the same way about life and its injustices. It is interesting, too, that they began to suffer increasingly from life's vicissitudes as the end of the century approached. Iriarte would die in 1791, quite young, decrying the career of letters and the troubles it brought. Meléndez, after entering the judicial field in 1789, would find that his life had taken indeed a new direction with many unexpected results, often disastrous in the extreme.

In addition to his intervention in the University community, whether it concerned the University or the town, Meléndez continued to write his poetry. After his first public appearances in 1780 and 1781, his popularity continued to grow. Some of this interest could have resulted from the indirect influence of Jovellanos and his timely introductions. Demerson includes in his study a note from the Duchess of Benavente, who was very active in the literary world of her day. In her letter dated Barcelona, July 9, 1783, she laments the delayed arrival of some unedited poems by Meléndez.[39] The open interest in his work, of which the Duchess' note is only one example, plus Jovellanos' prodding pushed Meléndez to publish his complete works. The first volume appeared in 1785.

This small volume was an immediate success. Sempere y Guarinos speaks of it very highly in 1787, quoting an Italian journal of July 23, 1785: " 'The poetry which we announce here indicates a renaissance [of Spanish letters] and a happy return to the sane, true principles of good taste which has always been in Spain, as well as in Italy, the basis for beautiful and pleasant literature.' " [40] This quotation is excellent proof of the new stature of the poet. His reputation before had been earned through poetic competitions, but now, because of a printed collection of his works, he was hailed as a poet of the first order, even as the restorer of Spanish poetry, by both Spanish and foreign critics. The only sour note was caused by his very success. Three or four unauthorized editions immediately followed the original. Meléndez' anger over this is probably what prevented his publishing a second volume which Sempere notes at some length, even citing the titles in it.[41] The 1785 edition, besides being somewhat rare, has thus the added distinction of never having been completed. Some of the poems in the proposed second volume were published later, either totally revised or slightly retouched. Some unfortunately have disappeared altogether.

In 1784 Meléndez gained some fame in the dramatic field, but it was short-lived. Eventually he was to wish he had never attempted such a public exhibition of his talents. To celebrate the recent peace treaty with England, which had also given the United States its beginning, and the birth of twin heirs to the Spanish throne, the city of Madrid held a literary contest. Two dramatic pieces were to be selected for presentation in the capital's two public theaters—La Cruz and El Príncipe. One condition was that from the day of the announcement the entries were to be in the judges' hands within sixty days. Meléndez was intrigued by the news. The competition neatly fitted into the development of his own work. Since 1777 he had been thinking of an episode in Spanish literature which he thought would lend itself to dramatic presentation. On October 6, 1777, he had written to Jovellanos: "The plan of the wedding of Camacho the Wealthy pleased me [. . . .] I found nothing in it that is not of a delicate taste. It follows the unities perfectly, and it truly deserves to be treated in verse [. . . .]" [42]

The project over the years had continued in the back of his mind, and with the news of the contest he set to work. He soon submitted his pastoral play *Las bodas de Camacho el rico* (*The Wedding of the Wealthy Camacho*). From this auspicious beginning, his play was to plummet to an ignominious end. When it was presented at the Cruz, it was completely rejected by the audience. The rejection was not so much due to the theme itself as to the incompatibility of content and structure. The episode comes from Part II of *Don Quixote*, Chapters XX and XXI. The characters there are realistic, as only Cervantes could present them. Meléndez put them in an idyllic Arcadian world. While in general the language in the play is beautiful, the fact that it is the original characters of the novel who speak this idealized language and live in this fantasied world caused an incongruousness that the audience could not accept. Had Meléndez chosen a different source for his play, the difficulties that occurred most likely would have been avoided. One should also remember that the basic interpretation of *Don Quixote* by eighteenth-century readers was still essentially a humorous one. The contrast of the at times bawdy humor in the novel no doubt tinged a reader's, or viewer's in this case, interpretation of any isolated episode. Indeed, very few defenses of the novel as having spiritual, ethereal significance had been made by the 1780's. One, curiously enough, was uttered by Cadalso. The Ríos and Bowle editions too had only just appeared—in 1780 and 1781.

Meléndez never again publicly presented any of his theatrical endeavors. Demerson has unearthed two embryonic works that may indicate that *The Wedding of the Wealthy Camacho* was not his only attempt to write a play. The first work is simply a brief plan for a plot which Demerson says recalls both *El delincuente honrado* (*The Honorable Culprit*) by Jovellanos and Lope's *El mejor alcalde el rey* (*The Best Mayor Is the King*). Somewhat more developed is a sketch of another dramatic project that deals with a Spanish historical figure, *María la brava*. The subject matter is similar to that in *Romeo and Juliet*. It is possible that Meléndez could have been influenced in the choice of subject by the English play because he did have the works of Shakespeare in his library. Demerson believes that the play, or the effort to write it, probably dates from the 1770's when Meléndez was greatly under the influence of Jovellanos. The play was evidently intended to be a Neoclassic tragedy in five acts.[43]

An epic poem, "La caída de Luzbel" ("The Fall of Lucifer"), was written around 1785 for the Royal Academy literary competition. It, too, was of earlier inspiration, coming from the time in the 1770's when Meléndez was actively studying Milton's *Paradise Lost*. The poem did not win a prize. From this time until he left Salamanca, Meléndez seems to have slowed down in his literary production. His fifth epistle to his friend Gaspar González de Cándamo, and his first discourse, "La despedida del anciano" ("The Farewell of the Old Man"), date from 1786–1787. In 1787 his philosophical ode "El deseo de gloria en los profesores de las artes" ("The Desire For Glory by Professors of the Arts") appeared. This poem was sent to the Academy of St. Ferdinand and read at its distribution of awards on July 14, 1787.

The atmosphere at Salamanca, of which we have seen several indications, had begun to weigh heavily upon Meléndez by the late 1780's. The acrimony and backbiting that he began to encounter in the midst of his fame, incompatible but intimate companions always, were becoming less and less acceptable to him. His only outstanding literary venture at this time was to enter into collaboration with two other professors in an attempt to publish several works, one of which was Cadalso's CARTAS MARRUECAS (*Moroccan Letters*). Meléndez added some letters of his own that were called *Cartas de Ibrahim* (*Letters From Ibrahim*) or *Cartas turcas* (*Turkish Letters*) written between 1780 and 1787. Meléndez' *Ensayo sobre la propiedad* (*Essay on Property*) was another of the works. The petition for publication was dated December 6, 1788.[44]

From January to June, 1789, Meléndez was in Madrid. Probably he went there to lobby for his new cause. By the 1788–1789 academic year he had definitely decided to leave the profession of teaching. As we have stated before, he had begun some time earlier to consider leaving. In addition to his growing displeasure with the university scene, he was pushed by his inherent desire to press on, to stand out. His career as a student, which was divided between the Humanities and Law, is enough to show the pull that both fields exerted on him. One might say that his decision was the result of an evolvement that had been going on for nearly twenty years, since the day he first entered the University of Salamanca in 1772. On May 22, 1789,[45] Meléndez was notified of his nomination as magistrate in the Criminal Court of Aragon in Zaragoza. From June until the end of August he was in Salamanca at the University, and on September 1 or 2, 1789, he left for Zaragoza.

IV *Meléndez' Legal Career*

On September 15 [46] Meléndez officially took up his duties as magistrate. There is little real evidence about the year and a half he spent in Zaragoza. Quintana presents virtually nothing although Navarrete, in his unedited *Noticia* (*Notice*), cited frequently by Demerson, gives some insight into how the new law officer went about carrying out his duties. Navarrete writes:

"His attendance in the courtroom was continuous and punctual as well as his zeal to give ear to private quarrels and his interest in resolving them amicably [. . . .] He listened to everyone with love, and with gentleness and persuasion reconciled their differences. His house was always open to litigants and those in need. He visited the jails to get the prisoners' testimony within twenty-four hours in order to alleviate their discomfort as much as possible, consoling them in their travails and not adding to these latter by appearing to be a stern, severe judge [. . . .] He patrolled until dawn not only his own quarter but at times two or three others because of his associates' illness. It happened once that Meléndez came upon an acquaintance in a gaming house, and after having had the money counted, which he had the bailiff pick up, he told the young acquaintance to come home with him and that, if he did not have a servant, he would accompany him, as he did. This offer made with the greatest urbanity and attention was as embarrassing and shameful for the young man as it was useful for his correction. The following morning Meléndez disposed of the money collected the night before as the law requires. Two thousand *reales* had been seized. Only two days before a prisoner had been executed who left behind a young widow with six children. Moved by her plight Meléndez had her brought before him, comforted her in her affliction, and told her how she should educate her children so they would not follow in the steps of their father. He ordered his secretary to count out the two thousand *reales* and to give them to the widow so she would have something to live on for a while at least." [47]

In the spring of 1791 Meléndez moved to Valladolid where he had been appointed a new judge. Even though in the short time he spent in Zaragoza he wrote little poetry, he had learned to be a good magistrate and certainly went beyond the call of duty, if Navarrete's statements are any indication. He had gained many new friends outside the purely literary and academic sphere which he had principally inhabited before. In his work with the Economic Society in Zaragoza he put into practice many of his basic precepts about the improvement of man's environment. Even more important for him was the proof that he could function well in this new life he had chosen.

In the beginning of 1792 the government sent him to oversee the unification of five small hospitals in Ávila. Actually this was a sort of persecution of Meléndez because his close friend and adviser, Jovellanos, had recently fallen from political favor. As is always the case in politics, the friends of the unfortunate one suffer his disgrace too. Jovellanos, who was just as impetuous as Meléndez when he saw an injustice being committed, had rallied to the defense of his friend Francisco de Cabarrús, the future founder of Spain's first national bank. In 1790 this man was imprisoned for alleged financial wrongdoings. Jovellanos was greatly disturbed at his friend's misfortune and sought to help him. His actions drew down upon him the opprobrium of more influential men, some of whom were his enemies, and he was ordered off to Asturias to look into the problems of roads and coal mines. He remained in this sort of semiexile for the next seven years.

Meléndez' persecution was in a way more difficult, although it came to him indirectly. Jovellanos was able to carry out many innovative projects in his native province and produced some of his most significant writings. Meléndez, on the other hand, found his task in Ávila unbearable, principally because of the political conniving he encountered there. Each of the hospitals intended to remain as independent as possible, and the officials were little disposed to look upon Meléndez with great favor. The chaos and furor that the petty bickering created caused him many problems. Twice he was seriously ill. Finally, the government allowed him to return to his judicial post at Valladolid even though Jovellanos still remained in Asturias.

In this appointment at Valladolid, as in the previous one, Meléndez did not write a great deal of new poetry. Most of his literary efforts involved the polishing of poems he had written earlier. This habit of his, which did not always improve the quality of his work, eventually became a constant fixation with him. In the early 1790's his polishing and revising were done with the idea of bringing out a definitive edition of his work. Naturally he regretted the events that had prevented a complete edition in 1785. The spurious editions and his own popularity goaded him on now in his intentions.

In these early years of the last decade of the century he had other projects in mind, too. One very important scheme was the establishment of a review that would encompass all branches of human knowledge in its coverage and show the state and progress of such knowledge in all civilized countries. This grandiose project, highly laudable in its intentions, was probably an attempt to overcome the stultifying effect the beginning years of Charles IV's reign had on the advancement of letters and the sciences in Spain. There was an almost total prohibition against both national and foreign reviews until Manuel Godoy became Prime Minister in 1792 and lightened censorship restrictions considerably. Meléndez and five other men of letters thought to take advantage of this freer atmosphere and publish their encyclopedic journal which would be called *El académico* (*The Academician*). By the early summer of 1793, the journal's state of organization was such that it could be given to the censors for their examination. However, upon receipt of the censors' demands, which were very severe, the editors halted any further development of their project. The historian Rafael Altamira says it was Godoy himself who effectively killed the project. One supposes the Prime Minister was not too eager to inform the public so liberally as the editors would have liked. Altamira writes: "Godoy was not so harsh as his predecessors, permitting the publication of the *Correo mercantil de España e Indias* (*Mercantile Mail of Spain and the Indies*) and others. He refused, on the other hand, to allow Meléndez Valdés, Clemencín, and several other writers to bring out an encyclopedic journal which was to be entitled *The Academician* [. . . .]" [48]

From about this time on, Meléndez involved himself more and more openly in politics, creating enemies for himself who would later cause his downfall. The poet wrote his philosophical ode XXIII on fanaticism at this time. References to the Inquisition, lightly veiled here, are even less covert in the first epistle, written to congratulate Godoy on his winning peace in 1795. These poems are discussed in our Chapters 3 and 4. With a clever mixture of astuteness and idealism, he wrote another epistle, number VII, to Godoy which Demerson calls "the manifesto of enlightened despotism in favor of the peasant class." [49] By now Meléndez was thoroughly aligned on the minister's side and, as a consequence, began incurring the wrath of the minister's enemies who were considerable in number.

With Meléndez' increased political activity and resultant problems, he postponed the new publication of his poetry until 1797. It was printed in Valladolid in three volumes and was dedicated to Godoy. This dedication placed Meléndez in a delicate and vulnerable political position. Jovellanos, it seems, was instrumental in Meléndez' maneuver and had been after him for some time to dedicate the work to the minister in order to gain his favor.

A few words are necessary at this point concerning Meléndez' political maneuverings. The most noticeable feature is again Meléndez' lack of hesitation in pushing his own cause. His manner of operations might at first seem devious, but is not really so. He simply finds the repressive atmosphere of the time intolerable, and realizes that by protesting it in the name of the Prime Minister his views will have more influence. There is not necessarily any idea of cold, impersonal politics involved. The lack of ruthless political motivation can be seen quite easily in Meléndez' horror at his embroilment in the polemics and bitter attacks that began coming his way. Unwittingly and somewhat naïvely, he became enmeshed in all the backbiting that he had always sought to escape—first in the University, almost immediately in his new legal career when he became involved with the hospitals in Ávila, and then increasingly in these politico-literary activities of the mid-nineties.

In the midst of the storm that began to form around him, Meléndez received word on October 3, 1797,[50] of his new appointment as District Attorney of Madrid. At the end of 1797, Meléndez had thus reached a peak in his life not altogether unlike those earlier ones in 1780–1781 and 1785. This one is important in that it is the last time he achieves any degree of universal popularity until long after his death.

The newest edition of his poetry placed him definitively at the top of the contemporary Spanish Parnassus. In 1798 he was elected to the Royal Academy of the Language. Because of political intrigue, however, he was prevented from taking his seat until September 10, 1810.[51]

His new judicial post allowed him to stay in the capital where he had always wanted to live. (The desire for bucolia, therefore, which we shall see in his poetry, hardly went hand in hand with the activities of his real life.) It is quite easy, then, to picture Meléndez in 1797. Believing Spain to be on the verge of a new literary reawakening, he felt that he would have a leading part in it, while following the other direction in his life, his legal career. In this year, therefore, he must have looked forward to a rosy future. Goya painted his portrait at this time, probably just before the announcement of his new judicial post. The painting, now in the Bowes Museum, Barnard Castle, Yorkshire, England, shows a face tired, grave, and prematurely aged. It is prophetic of the misfortunes that Meléndez was to suffer in his remaining years.

At first this period in Meléndez' life started off very promisingly. Meléndez began his new work in February. Navarrete's report is helpful in showing more personal details of what he was doing:

"He immediately began to carry out his duties. His predecessor José Álvarez Baragaña was quite old and ill, and for this reason Meléndez found the backlog of work tremendous. He worked with great energy to bring everything up to date, and, since he did everything himself, his subordinate [. . .] said that he had never seen a man like him who left nothing for him to do nor asked anything of him. His clerk, N. Pastor said the same thing seeing him work night and day. Indeed, in the silence of the night he found the greatest relief and comfort. 'The quiet of the night,' he said, 'is best for working.' After having worked all morning he would go at two-thirty to visit his close friend Mr. Jovellanos (then Minister of Justice), would then return home, eat, rest for a half hour, retire to read, work in his study, return in the evening for another half hour with Mr. Jovellanos, and then until dinnertime he would shut himself up in his office. In the short time that he was District Attorney, he handled serious cases of all sorts. His handling of these cases, of which the public has probably heard, is an excellent testimony to his fine judgment, learning, and sense of duty." [52]

What happened to Meléndez for the next several years was influenced again by what happened to Jovellanos, just as in the early nineties. The political machinations that endlessly went on show very well the essential instability of this period. Cabarrús, who had been the indirect reason for Jovellanos' exile originally, eventually regained court favor and worked to bring back Jovellanos. In 1797, quite without warning, the latter was named ambassador to Russia. Then, before he set out for his new post, he was named Minister of Justice. This nervous sort of functioning of the government could turn to another, more negative extreme just as quickly. On March 28, 1798, Godoy supposedly retired from active participation in the government. He still exerted a great deal of influence and continued to intervene in matters of state, which greatly bothered Jovellanos, who, along with one or two others in responsible positions, suffered the consequences of any mistakes. Very soon his worry became unbearable, and he retired from his post after a very short-lived return to grace. His enemies had even bribed one of his servants to poison him. Jovellanos was saved and, as if obviously escaping from the too real world, he returned to Asturias in August, 1798.[53] His fall or retirement brought with it the demise of friends' political careers. Meléndez thus found himself relieved of his official duties on August 27, 1798. He was ordered to leave for Medina del Campo within twenty-four hours and to wait there for further orders.

On October 6, 1798, Meléndez' semibanishment from the capital was softened through the intervention of friends on his behalf. He was given the duty of inspecting the construction of some new barracks and to supervise the public lands and excise taxes in Medina. He took a great interest in the hospital there, this being less a chore since he was genuinely concerned about this sort of charitable work. He was occupied in these pursuits until 1800. He still continued officially as the District Attorney of Madrid because he had not been dismissed from the post, only temporarily relieved of his duties. But the notice of retirement came officially on December 3, 1800. His salary was cut fifty percent and he was ordered to transfer to Zamora. There he was to report to the Captain General and was not to leave the city without the permission of the King. To add further misery to the situation, Meléndez fell ill with a severe fever that only gradually yielded to treatment. Because of constant worry over his precarious position, his physical state was never strong anyway. His doctor wrote to Madrid stating that the jurist could hardly leave for Zamora in his present condition. Meléndez, after recovering his strength somewhat, wrote the King, asking why he was being retired when he was still in his prime and could be of great service to the government. No response was made to either of these letters until March 2, 1801, when the King granted Meléndez permission to stay in Medina until he had sufficiently recovered his health. On March 29 a letter came from the Ministry of Justice, ordering him to obey the original command at once and go to Zamora. As soon as possible Meléndez dejectedly set off for that city. In Zamora he lived quietly and worked according to the dictates of his literary inspiration.

In September and October of 1801 he finally discovered some of the reasons for the unhappy turn in his life. Friends in Madrid had been investigating and were able to piece the story together. His enemies, it seemed, were determined to disgrace Meléndez completely. To discredit him, these enemies ordered the Vicar of Madrigal, a village on the outskirts of Medina, to prefer charges against the *Corregidor* of the town. Meléndez was to be involved in these charges if at all possible. The Vicar thus complained to the Bishop of the Diocese of Ávila of the conduct of the *Corregidor*, Andrés Quintana. The Bishop called in the two priests of the town to tell what they knew of the *Corregidor's* activities, specifically asking whether Meléndez and he were good friends. They were questioned as to whether the civil official had a mistress and a child by her, whether Quintana had said this was not a sin, and whether he had been influenced by Meléndez in his attitudes. The questions were answered without implicating Meléndez in any way. The case was thought closed until the Bishop sent a full report to Madrid, whereupon Quintana was dismissed and Meléndez lost his position as District Attorney.

When Meléndez knew the facts of the sordid episode, he set out to fight the case against him. He wrote out a brief in favor of the two priests, who were also charged, which was presented by a friend before the ecclesiastical tribunal in Ávila. The friend brilliantly showed that the whole situation had no real basis in fact and had been brought about by jealously and hatred on the part of Meléndez' enemies. The friend wished to know why Meléndez had been brought into the case since he had nothing to do with local affairs. The brief, presented in late October, 1801, was strongly worded and asked for a dismissal of the indictments against all the defendants. It was not admitted as part of the trial records, but nevertheless the two priests were restored to their posts and the case was dropped. On June 27, 1802, Meléndez was restored to his full salary as District Attorney, and the restriction on his place of residence was removed.[54]

Meléndez now wanted to go to Madrid, his name and integrity being publicly vindicated. Friends advised against the move and he returned instead to Salamanca. Here he worked on arranging his huge library, which, according to his own statements, was one of the best in the country, and devoted time to literary parjects. A long poem about the creation based on Haydn's oratorio and a translation of the *Aeneid* were the main results of his activity. He continued in his habit of reworking his poetry, with the intention of publishing a selective edition of his works.

V *Return to Favor and Last Days*

Meléndez remained in Salamanca for six years. During this period the political situation of Spain was in constant upheaval. The intrigue that we have already noted was in great part a result of the unsettled state in the rest of Europe. The domination of France over Spain was indirect in the 1790's, but when Napo-

leon overthrew the Directory in 1799 French influence became
more overt. The relations between Godoy and Napoleon were
never very good and this caused much trouble for Spain. The
French had been greatly responsible for Godoy's retirement in
1797, and in Spain the public opposition to Godoy tended to
gravitate toward Charles IV's son, the future Ferdinand VII.
Napoleon cultivated this opposition to thwart Godoy at every
turn. A successful campaign against Portugal in 1807 allowed
thousands of French troops into Spain, and through deceit they
began to take over the northern sections of the country. Godoy
saw what was happening and favored the withdrawal of the
French troops. Charles IV, as weak and vacillating as ever, was
afraid to invite the wrath of Napoleon and so opposed any show
of force. The Emperor now asked for the cession of certain Spanish provinces in the north as far as the Ebro. The King belatedly
regretted his vacillation. He saw escape to the Spanish colonies in
America as his only recourse and moved the court from Madrid
to Aranjuez as a preliminary step. Ferdinand, even more duped
than his father, still continued blindly attached to Napoleon. A
riot occurred in Aranjuez on March 17 and 18, 1808, in which
Godoy was captured by the followers of Ferdinand and was barely
saved from death. Realizing that the army and the people were
on the side of Ferdinand, Charles abdicated on March 19. The
greatly beloved Prince—and how vain such love was to prove
later when he finally did reign—now came to the throne.

Napoleon was not much pleased with the course of events
because he had never intended making Ferdinand king. Forced
to show his real intentions, he managed to do so in a brilliant
manner, showing his own extreme intelligence and the stupidity
of both Charles and Ferdinand. Napoleon had his general, Murat,
enter Madrid with an army on March 23. On the next day Ferdinand made his royal entry and was jubilantly received by the
people. All foreign diplomats, except the French, recognized the
new King. Napoleon was still uncertain as to how best pursue
his plans, but Charles unwittingly helped him. To save his family
he communicated with Murat and secretly retracted his abdication, placing himself entirely in the hands of the Emperor. In the
meantime, Murat told Ferdinand that the Emperor was coming
to see him and suggested that he go to meet him at Burgos.
Ferdinand, after much hesitation, not only went to Burgos but,

not finding Napoleon there, went across the border to Bayonne. He did find Napoleon there—and was duly informed that he would have to abdicate. A few days later, on April 30, Charles, the Queen María Luisa, and Godoy also arrived, having been persuaded by Murat to go there. This reunion was a disgraceful one for the Spanish royal family because of the violent quarrels which erupted among its members, all in the presence of Napoleon. Both father and son were definitively forced to abdicate, and Napoleon was given the right to name a new King of Spain.

In Madrid, as well as in other parts of the country, there was great hostility toward the French troops who had been conducting themselves like the victors after a battle. The climax came when an order arrived from Napoleon for the rest of the royal family to be sent to France. The departure from Madrid was set for the morning of May 2. A crowd gathered to see the royal party off. Rumors began to circulate and the people soon began to insult the French soldiers. A French batallion appeared and fired into the crowd without warning. The news spread over the city like wildfire, and a general uprising ensued. The battle lasted several hours and the French, superior in numbers and arms, were victorious. The events of the *dos de mayo* were to have lasting psychological and emotional effects on the people and were politically to inaugurate a different Spain from the one that had existed for centuries.[55]

When Meléndez returned to the capital in 1808, as we can see, it hardly was a propitious time to become involved in public life again. Meléndez did not really appear too anxious to return at first. On April 2 Meléndez wrote Ferdinand thanking him for favors in his behalf, but even after being offered another judicial post he chose to remain in the peace and quiet of Salamanca. Pressed further by the government, he soon did go to the capital. Here he wrote his patriotic poem, his first "Alarma española" ("Spanish Alarm"), inciting his compatriots to arms against the French. He, in a way, was thus one of the initiators of the events of the *dos de mayo*. Then on May 17 he received a notice to proceed to Oviedo to investigate uprisings there. Meléndez agreed to this assignment and set off soon after. Many of his critics have never really forgiven him this apparent "treason" against his country—i.e., to investigate his own countrymen.

The events in Spain since Charles IV's abdication had kept

the entire citizenry in a state of nervous energy. With the news of the events in the capital on May 2, the people in the very northern province of Asturias became increasingly restless and rose up in revolt on May 9. Murat sent in soldiers to quell the uprising. At the same time the *Junta Central*, the governing body left in control by Ferdinand before his departure from the capital, ordered two magistrates to Oviedo to look into the situation. These two were the Count of Pinar and Meléndez Valdés. It should be emphasized that they were not sent by the French general, but by the Spanish governing body, the *Junta*. The purpose of their trip has at times been carelessly explained. They were not sent to prosecute their countrymen, but to look over matters there, calm the atmosphere if possible, and report back to the *Junta*.

While they were on their way to Oviedo, another uprising occurred in Oviedo. On the night of May 24, all the bells of the city began ringing at midnight, the signal for a general outpouring of anger against the invaders. The rebels took over one arsenal and captured one hundred thousand rifles, and on the morning of May 25 the people of Asturias declared war on Napoleon.[56] It was toward this chaotic, dangerous situation that the two emissaries of the national government were headed.

When the Count and Meléndez reached their destination, a mob overtook their carriage and carried them off prisoners to Oviedo. They succeeded in proving their innocence to the local governing body, but the mob outside, thirsting for blood and revenge on somebody, captured them again. After some delay, the two victims were taken to a field to be shot. Meléndez attempted to inject some reason and calm into the mad scene but was not successful. A great deal of time passed, during which the prisoners were tied up twice, the second time so they could be shot in the back as traitors. At this climactic point, heightening the effect of this very real drama, a religious procession descended upon the scene. Everyone knelt in reverence at the sight of the Sacrament and the locally famous Cross of Victory. This action brought a degree of sanity to the mob. The prisoners at length were untied and taken back to town. At another trial held to satisfy the people, Meléndez and the Count of Pinar were again acquitted. They did manage to reach Madrid this time.[57]

This episode must have been one of the most degrading Meléndez ever experienced. And yet, when he returned to Madrid in August, 1808, he was to start another high period in his life. His activities between 1808 and 1813 involved him in the center of the political and social sphere of Joseph Bonaparte, the new King of Spain. Many people have faulted Meléndez for this new "treason." Yet, as we have seen before, we find once again that Meléndez was staying close to a median way in his life—to what he thought best for the betterment of his country. If his concept of national betterment went hand in hand with his ideas about personal advancement, we should not be unduly alarmed. I do not believe there is any of the selfishness and vacillating deviousness in him at this point that critics have sometimes ascribed to him.

Meléndez at first waited for a post from the *Junta Central* which was in control after the decisive defeat of the French in the battle of Bailén on June 23, 1808. But the Spaniards were unable to create any sense of harmony among themselves, and that winter Napoleon entered Madrid at the head of sixty thousand troops. Joseph returned to the capital on January 22, 1809.[58] There were now about three hundred thousand French soldiers in Spain. The *Junta* fled first to Seville and then Cádiz. Meléndez remained in the capital.

With the return of Joseph, Meléndez' fortunes experienced an immediate change for the better. A decree was promulgated on February 6, 1809, which set up two Councils or *Juntas* composed of ten judges, five on each Council. Meléndez was named one of the members. His membership also provided him entry into the most socially prominent salons. At the beginning of 1809, then, Meléndez achieved certain ends he had been pursuing all his life. It is ironic, and unfortunate for his later reputation, that these achievements came under a government that would always be considered inimical to the true Spanish spirit, an ironic result in itself largely due to the vociferous Romantics of the 1830's.

The most outstanding case in which Meléndez became very publicly involved was the González-Luquede affair. Demerson goes into some detail in his Chapter Fourteen on this matter which is important for showing what Meléndez was doing at this time, a period that earlier biographers have only sketched, and for showing that Meléndez, as always, was determined to see the fair execution of the law. The case involved a couple who had been in litigation for ten years. The young woman, Manuela

González, had decided she did not wish to marry the man, Hilario Luquede, to whom she had been betrothed. The case had been before civil and ecclestical courts without ever being resolved. Meléndez became involved when the case came before the Council. He attacked the problem at the essence of its absurdity —that the Spanish court system needed overhauling. He believed that the ecclestical courts, which consistently had ruled in favor of the hopeful bridegroom, had no jurisdiction in such matters. Indeed, by ruling in favor of the girl, he was recommending that the Church return to its original, primitive mission—i.e., a spiritual one. Meléndez' enlightened attitude which had so staunchly favored the principles and actions of Charles III, and which had always stood up in favor of Jovellanos, had not been lost or dismissed. His decision here is that of the Spanish *ilustrado* at his most intelligent, reasoned, and, not least, sensitive. The Council, because of divisions among its members, ruled finally that it was not supposed to decide such a matter and that the girl should take her case elsewhere. The general feeling of the Council was therefore hardly as advanced as that of Meléndez. Nevertheless, several months after Meléndez had had his recommendation brought to the King's attention, a decree was issued which restored to civil magistrates all the civil jurisdiction formerly held by the ecclesiastical magistrates.[59] We do not know exactly what role Meléndez played in this achievement, but it is noteworthy that he was soon placed on the Council of State. Not long after, he was made a member of the Civil Law Board, the Board of Public Education, and the Finance Board. He was also named to the Board of the Theater, a more literary endeavor than the others with which he was involved. This board, set up by Joseph, was to act as a sort of screening process before dramas could be presented. Although virtually nothing is known of Meléndez' participation, the existence of the board proves that the drama was still not in the state of artistic perfection that had been sought since the mid-eighteenth century by the Neoclassicists.

Between 1808 and 1813, Meléndez' general social situation changed. He moved about in the highest circles. Concomitant with his new position, his financial picture greatly improved. He took part once again in the functioning of the Academy of St. Ferdinand and the Royal Academy of the Language, to which he had been named in 1798 but which he was unable to enter officially until September 11, 1810. On December 23, 1809, he was named a member of the Royal Order of Spain. He was also declared a member of the National Institute. These positions, whether actively engaged in or not, are significant as a picture of the renown and prestige enjoyed by the jurist-poet in the period of Napoleonic rule in Spain. They have a kind of poignant effect on us, however, because they were so ephemeral. They occurred at a time in Spain's history that aroused much resentment in succeeding decades. All those associated with the Napoleonic group in power were largely denounced by later generations. Meléndez' advantageous situation, in this light, seems quite empty. While his reputation would be rehabilitated more quickly than those of most of his contemporaries involved in the French-inclined government, this period in his life might have been better spent outside the French-dominated sphere even though he did effect a great deal in advancing the interpretation of Spanish law. The five-year period for his own actual good might be considered, however, quite hollow and ineffectual in the long run because the positive state he found himself in at the moment quickly became a most negative one.

Demerson has discovered one last, short-lived office to which Meléndez was appointed. In May, 1812, he was named President of the Prefectorial Board of Segovia. This was an important position in itself, since this board, as other similar ones throughout the country, had the responsibility of carrying out on a local level all decrees, laws, or plans formulated by the central government in Madrid. The board was somewhat unnecessary in 1812, however, because of the impoverished state of the Bonaparte government. Meléndez seems not to have taken up residence in Segovia until mid-July because of delays by the government in sending him to his new post. His stay was not long, either. Joseph came to the city around July 30, and Meléndez almost certainly returned with him to Madrid on August 3.[60] Meléndez probably could have done much good in the post, which he filled for all of two and one-half months, under propitious circumstances.

Meléndez' short stay in Segovia and his hurried return to the capital were indicative of what would happen to him until he at last was safe in exile in France, after having followed Joseph and his government there. On August 10, a large convoy of

French and some Spaniards set out from Madrid. The military picture was so bad in Spain by this time—Napoleon's own fall would not be too far away—that the central government could not control the deteriorating situation. Madrid was fully evacuated on August 12. The convoys eventually merged and ended up in Valencia. It appears that Meléndez was among these people who went to Valencia since Demerson has found a reference to his being there.⁶¹ On September 10, a new convoy was prepared to go to the north. Although many of Meléndez' friends joined it, he did not. He preferred to stay in Valencia, hoping somehow to be able to return to Madrid.

Joseph regained the capital in early 1813, and Meléndez was in a convoy that reached Madrid on February 14. He was to stay there until May 25, when the final order of evacuation came. Again Meléndez was among the émigrés because he realized that to stay could mean death for him. He was forced to leave his possessions behind. Even worse for him was the knowledge that his home in Salamanca had been sacked and burned. The convoy rather precipitately reached the French border as the fighting closed in behind. For the Spaniards their entry into France was an emotional one because they knew they had to enter or otherwise be captured and suffer severe punishment. In most cases they were leaving their homeland behind forever. Quintana, in a brief, moving paragraph, tells us how Meléndez entered his self-imposed exile: "Before entering France he knelt and kissed the Spanish earth, saying: 'I shall never walk on you again!' Then he remembered his home, his books, his friends, and his peaceful retreat that he had had there. Bitterly recalling his cruel fate which was now forcing him away from all he had achieved, tears fell from his eyes and were caught up in the Bidassoa." ⁶² We shall see these same emotions in more detail in Chapter Four as they reappear in the prologue written in Nîmes for the new edition of his works, and in the poem "El náufrago" ("The Shipwrecked Man"). Meléndez knew, and Quintana understood very well, that he would never see his homeland again and that he was in essence cutting himself off from what was his most intimate self.

Old and ill, Meléndez at first moved about from place to place in Southern France without ever settling down. After staying for a while in Toulouse and elsewhere, he settled in Montpellier. Meléndez chose this place for various reasons, it would seem—

the agreeable climate, the low cost of living, and the medical faculty at the University. He needed the latter for treatment of his rheumatism that had been bothering him for some time. Soon after his arrival in France he had also suffered a partial paralysis which could not be entirely cured. For long periods of time he could not use his right arm.

He was now sixty years old. Constant worry over his precarious financial state, his failure to get permission to return to Spain, the absence from friends, and, perhaps most important, a profound melancholy caused by the injustice of his situation made his physical recovery all the more impossible. All his ailments, physical and emotional, undoubtedly hurried his death which, had he been in more pleasant circumstances and in Spain, would have been delayed by his own constitution.

Unfortunately, Meléndez was not able to remain even in Montpellier. An order was promulgated by the French government that called for the dispersal of the Spanish exiles. Meléndez went first to Nîmes where he spent most of the year 1815. Here he worked on the new edition of his poetry he had been planning for some time. Most likely because of his illness and the need for medical care, Meléndez was allowed to return to Montpellier probably in early 1816. At his return he was able to rent a small lodging from a certain Dr. Fage. The care by this physician, the love of his wife, the warm climate of the area, and the thermal baths—cures which had not been very successful before—now began to take effect. By the beginning of May, 1817, he had almost regained his former health. He was able to walk about, and the physical recovery must have given him an emotional uplift. All seemed to be going, if not perfectly, at least better than ever before in this undesired exile. And then on May 24, 1817, the poet suddenly died. Doña María has left us the most intimate recital of his death: " 'On May, 1817 [. . .] at 9:11 P.M. God was served by calling my beloved Meléndez to him. He had spent the day in good spirits. He went to bed and told me: "Please bring me a cup of tea [. . . .]" It was immediately brought to him. On taking the first sip, he moved his head back and forth two or three times, raised it up, and then let it fall. It took no more than two minutes. He expired in my arms.' " [63] Dr. Fage asserted that while Meléndez had indeed suffered a stroke, he had been suf-

fering all along from a deficient diet occasioned by his impoverished state.

The peace and tranquility that Meléndez had so much desired
in his last years in exile were still not forthcoming after his death.
He was to be reinterred several times before reaching his final
resting place in the twentieth century. Meléndez' wife first got
a temporary burial spot not far from Montpellier. Doña María,
however, after vain efforts to get the Spanish government to transfer the body to Spain, began to worry because her husband had
not been buried in hallowed ground. A curate in the neighboring
town of Montferrier, a friend of the poet, was easily persuaded to
allow burial in his parish church. Doña María continued her
efforts to have the body returned to Spain. She was particularly
hopeful since the new liberal government was going to publish
his works. (This was the 1820 edition.) Doña María died in 1822,
and in 1823 French intervention destroyed the constitutional
government and restored Ferdinand VII to power. Further sale
of Meléndez' works was forbidden and the matter of reinterment
of his body in Spain was dropped. Meléndez was reinterred in
Montpellier on March 17, 1828, however, at the instigation of
former friends. An imposing stone sepulcher was erected with an
inscription. Then, in 1863, a movement was started to bring
Meléndez' body back to Spain. On December 5, 1865, a royal
decree was issued authorizing the Treasury to set aside sufficient
funds to cover the expense. On April 25, 1866, the body was
exhumed from its burial place in Montpellier, sent to Madrid, and
buried in the Church of San Isidro next to the remains of Donoso
Cortés and Leandro Fernández de Moratín.

This was still not to be the final burial. On July 31, 1884, a
royal decree was issued for the construction of a Pantheon of
Illustrious Men in the San Justo Cemetery in Madrid. It was to
contain Donoso Cortés, Meléndez Valdés, and Moratín. The
monument was finished in December, 1888. Then the government
decided to bring Goya's remains back from France. This was done
in 1889. Finally on May 11, 1900, the coffins of the four exiles
were placed in the new monument.[64] Even though these incredible
burials may seem grotesque, Meléndez after nearly a century had
at last received the grateful homage of his country.

CHAPTER 2

"Light" Poetry of Meléndez

I *The Salamancan School*

THE reader may be somewhat mystified at first by the title of this chapter. Critics, when discussing Meléndez' poetry, often refer to much of it as being light, airy, and of little real substance. They say that his Anacreontic poems, the principal source of their complaints, were products of his youth and are therefore a reflection of an immaturity and irresponsibility that his personality exuded. However, such critics conveniently forget that Meléndez wrote in the Anacreontic mode during his entire life. Indeed it is in these graceful, amatory poems that we find a basis for the assertion of Meléndez' importance as the restorer of Spanish lyric poetry in the second half of the eighteenth century. The title of our chapter is an ironic, even facetious one therefore. We shall see that Meléndez' Anacreontic lyrics are quite important in the development of his total work. By studying them and others of his poems in comparison to different artistic manifestations of the century, we shall see, too, that his poetry is not at all alien, bizarre, or even unrealistic.

We have discussed Meléndez' career at the University of Salamanca rather fully in Chapter 1, but we did not go into the background of the people who formed a group later called the Salamancan or Salmantine School of Poetry. This title is a direct linkage to the more famous sixteenth-century group of poets known by the same name. The nucleus of eighteenth-century poets at Salamanca held sway as arbiters of poetic taste in the 1770's and 1780's. Forming the core of this eighteenth-century Salamancan School of Poets were three students and three Augustine clerics, of the same order as the leader of the sixteenth-century School, Fray Luis de León. The three clerics were Diego Tadeo González (Delio), Juan Fernández de Rojas (Liseno), and Andrés del Corral (Andrenio). The students were José Iglesias de la Casa (Arcadio), Juan Pablo Forner (Amintas), and Meléndez Veldés (Batilo). Forner's nature was too polemical to allow him to remain a conscious member of the group for long. Nicasio Álvarez de Cienfuegos and Manuel José Quintana are also considered members of the group although they were much younger than the others. Cienfuegos, after Meléndez, is perhaps the most outstanding lyric poet of the eighteenth century. Quintana lived long into the nineteenth century and, while an ardent disciple of Meléndez in his youth particularly, later wrote rhetorical, nationalistic poetry more in tone with his and his country's attitudes in the new century.

As we implied in Chapter 1 when noting Cadalso's influence on the early background of Meléndez, Cadalso, whose poetic epithet was Dalmiro, served as the solidifier of the group when he came to Salamanca in 1773. All the poets of the group followed the tenets of the Neoclassic school with its dual emphasis on utility and pleasure, the Horatian *utile dulci.* Like the Spanish Neoclassic writers in general, they looked for inspiration in outstanding writers of Spain's Golden Age. The influence of the sixteenth-century writers, particularly Garcilaso de la Vega and Fray Luis de León, was therefore just as important as that of Horace. This nationalistic tendency of eighteenth-century Spanish men of letters was their most distinguishing characteristic. The members of the Salamancan School did not always exhibit a certain formality seen at times in some Neoclassic poets. They did not necessarily reject any aims of the Neoclassicists, but rather amplified them to include currently developing attitudes and philosophies. Their poetry is thus quite diverse in form and outlook: tender, bucolic, sensual, melancholy, sentimental, philosophical, social, and at times even political.

Diego González, the unofficial leader of the group, was born in 1733 and quite early saw in Fray Luis de León his model for writing poetry. He began to write in the *lira,* the poetic form introduced into Spain by Garcilaso and then perfected by Fray Luis in the second half of the sixteenth century. More important for the development of a poetic style and attitude for himself and his followers was González' emphasis on decorum, simple elegance, and harmony of the subject and its treatment in his poems.

JUAN MELÉNDEZ VALDÉS

These characteristics are particularly evident in Fray Luis's poetry. As we might expect, Meléndez, the direct disciple of both González and of Fray Luis, very nicely evidences them also.

When Cadalso arrived in Salamanca in May, 1773, he was much taken with the attitude of this small group of poets, an attitude that was so different from the generally repressive one of the University as a whole. He was especially impressed with the youthful exuberance and sensitivity of Meléndez. As we saw in Chapter 1 briefly, Cadalso's travels and resultant sophistication were naturally attractive to Meléndez. The appeal of a new and foreign world with its different outlooks and philosophies almost immediately began to take hold in Meléndez' mind. Changes in his outlook began to appear so that what might have been at first a purely Neoclassic attitude became more open and less unyielding. An incipient "Romantic" attitude manifests itself from a very early point in his literary career, we may say. From his first days as a poet to his death, we find him following a dual path in his writing of poetry. A "Classical" attitude is exhibited in his imitations of Horace, in the writing itself of Anacreontics, and in the use of Classical metrical forms such as the ode. Yet within this very writing, he expresses very personal themes and he begins to include new eighteenth-century philosophies in the Anacreontics themselves. And at the same time he is searching for old and different Classical meters, he looks for purely Spanish ones to enrich his poetic expression. The eventual, almost excessive cultivation of the *romance* is a good example.

Ignacio de Luzán, who established the basic premises of the Spanish Neoclassicists, held that pleasure was principally an intellectual one since it was derived from studying models, themselves based on nature. With this search for models, particularly from the 1500's, went a revived interest in the pastoral mode of that time, a mode itself in imitation of an Antique genre. This revived interest, in an elementary but blatant way, is seen in the use of Arcadian names by the Salamancan poets. It is moreover a good indication of the poets' inherent desire for a renovation of poetic expression. Even more important is that, in itself, the use of Arcadian names emphasizes the poets' insistence on a personal touch and a closeness with nature which immediately set them off from the other, more formal Neoclassicists. The more immediate longing for nature, for physical contact with her, eventually carried the School beyond the tenets of Luzán and pure Spanish Neoclassicism.

Meléndez, during the 1770's, began to withdraw from a total commitment to Neoclassical precepts. Luzán's formulas, to be sure, were still active in guiding his creative abilities, but they were subjected to a secondary position. The inherent sensitivity of the poet's personality became responsible for a more intimate, personal outlook. It is at this point that he can be best compared to Tomás de Iriarte, who so well represents the Spanish Neoclassicist of the times. Iriarte had feelings, naturally, but his aesthetic criteria would not permit him to express them openly. He expressed a more reserved attitude that is seemingly cold, until we realize that it is not so much he himself who is cold, but rather the sense of propriety and formality of the Neoclassic school that holds him back. Meléndez, had he possessed the desire for control that Iriarte possessed, would have been little different from his contemporary. But Meléndez, because of his inherently sensitive nature and his readings of English and French writers, set forth on a divergent path from Iriarte's.[1] Meléndez eventually affirmed that the best form of artistic expression is that which communicates the artist's emotion directly to other men. Such expression meant the denuding of himself in his verse and ultimately made him vulnerable to both love and attack from his fellowman.

II *The Stated Attitude of Meléndez' Early Verses*

At the beginning of Meléndez' first edition of poetry in 1785, and in most later editions, there is a short poem entitled "A mis lectores" ("To My Readers"). It states what the attitude of all his poems supposedly will be. This poem, dating probably from the 1770's, admittedly has little of real seriousness in it. Nevertheless, it is imperative that we realize right away that the poet's attitude is not to be taken at face value. As we shall soon see, the frivolity and hedonism in this particular poem represent only the pleasant surface of what in its totality is very personal, profound poetry. I present the Spanish poem in its entirety with my own translation:

Not with my peaceful lyre
In sad laments
Will the fortunes be sung
Of unhappy kings;
Nor the cry of the soldier
Fierce in battle;
Nor the thunder with which
The horrible bronze spits
   forth its ball.
I tremble and shudder;
For inspiration does not permit
Tender lips
Such sublime songs.
I am a youth, and I want
To say more pleasant things
And delight myself
With dances and parties.
Crowned
With roses and gillyflowers,
With laughter and verses
I call out the toasts.
In chorus the girls
Join together to hear me,
And with great ardor
Repeat my songs;
Since Bacchus and Venus
Allowed me to be happy
And celebrate their glory
In sweet hymns.

(No con mi blanda lira
Serán en ayes tristes
Lloradas las fortunas
De reyes infelices;
Ni el grito del soldado,
Feroz en crudas lides;
O el trueno con que arroja
La bala el bronce horrible.

Yo tiemblo y me estremezco;
Que el numen no permite
Al labio temeroso
Canciones tan sublimes.
Muchacho soy, y quiero
Decir más apacibles
Querellas, y gozarme
Con danzas y convites.
En ellos coronado
De rosas y alhelíes,
Entre risas y versos
Menudeo los brindis.
En coros las muchachas
Se juntan por oírme,
Y al punto mis cantares
Con nuevo ardor repiten;
Pues Baco y el de Venus
Me dieron que felice
Celebre en dulces himnos
Sus glorias y festines.)[2]

The shortness of the verses—heptasyllabic, a favorite of Meléndez, with the strong accent on the sixth syllable—provides an important musicality to the structure of the poem. Assonance in the even-numbered lines adds to the regularity of the form. We can see here in an elemental way two essential characteristics of his poetry that captivated his audience—the regulated simplicity of the form and the musical freedom of the verses. These qualities further enhance the message—it itself being one of lyrical abandon and escape. The tone reflects somewhat the mood of Garcilaso's famous *Canción* V ("Si de mi baja lira [. . .]"). The closeness of the vocabulary in the first lines of both poems suggests a strong influence of the sixteenth-century poet on Meléndez during the early years of his writing. There is also in the tone of Meléndez' poem a source for the Modernist attitude at the end of the nine-teenth century.

Before we relegate Meléndez' poems to a limbo of artificiality, it would be well to note some of his prefatory remarks in the first edition. There is first a long dedicatory poem to Jovellanos, the man to whom Meléndez turned for paternal guidance partic-ularly after his brother's death in 1777. In the following brief quotation from the poem he refers specifically to Jovellanos' aid and even uses words reminiscent of San Juan de la Cruz' longing for a protector:

> Yes, you turned to me, when unknown
> And inert in a dark night
> My uncultured inspiration lay, your face
> With which you awaken talent and the arts.
> You extended your generous hand
> To pull me into the light, and my teacher,
> My father, and my friend you tried to be.[3]

In the last section of the poem, omitted here, he addresses himself to Friendship, who he hopes will make his poetry and the memory of Jovellanos and himself eternal. While the personifica-tion of friendship is not unusual, especially since the theme was ardently cultivated by all the poets of the Salamancan School, Meléndez' early desire for a kind of immortality is very important here. The expression of this desire nicely contradicts the effer-vescent superficiality in the first poem quoted above.

Also in the prefatory material of the 1785 edition is the *Ad-vertencia* written in prose. It contains certain ideas that show Meléndez to be far from the playful youth he presents in "To My Readers." In the first paragraph of the *Advertencia* he sounds very much like Iriarte in his distrust of critics. Meléndez is de-termined to defy his decriers: "The publication of these poems, in a time when ignorance and envy have united to discredit whatever poetry is published, is good proof that their author is not afraid of attacks. Indeed, just as he will receive with appre-ciation impartial judgments of people of good taste in order to correct himself where necessary, he will mock stupid, puerile criticisms made by some to whom his manner of writing is dis-agreeable."[4] He strongly defends his use of archaic words, a practice which was already being attacked by some of the more

[61]

ardent Neoclassicists, including Iriarte. Meléndez is really not much bothered by such criticisms: "In the use of *archaisms* or of antiquated words and locutions he [i.e., Meléndez] has not been very scrupulous. He quite definitely believes that they greatly contribute to maintaining the wealth and noble majesty of our language and that it is better to reestablish their use than to adopt other expressions of illegitimate [i.e., foreign] origin which disfigure and offend it." [5]

The tone we find in Meléndez' words is indicative of that throughout the preliminary material of the first edition. By no means does the author sound timid or withdrawing, but to the contrary. With such an attitude in mind, we should not place undue emphasis on the supposed goals enumerated in "To My Readers." On the surface, this youthful love poetry may seem airy, exuberant, and of little weight. Underneath, however, its bases are quite personal and serious.

III *The Anacreontic Mode*

In the various editions of Meléndez' poetry, the beginning poems are designated as "Odas anacreónticas" ("Anacreontic Odes"). There are only twenty-four of them in the 1785 edition, whereas their number is greatly increased in later publications. The mood of Anacreontic poetry was well suited to Meléndez' purposes as reiterated in "To My Readers." This type of poetry—gentle or boisterous in tone and varied in form—celebrates the love between two people. Sometimes, however, the love that the poetry depicts is not reciprocated and, as a result, the poet is provided the opportunity to bewail his desolate fate. Still, whether the poet has been fortunate or not in his love affairs, when he is declaiming his feelings for the beloved, he expresses himself with great exuberance. Meléndez expresses both the positive and negative attitudes in his verses. His use of the Anacreontic is part of that genre's long development throughout Western Europe. In Spain, Meléndez brings this type of poetry to its greatest achievement, not only in style but in popularity with the general Spanish public.

Such poetry received its name from Anacreon of Teos, who lived from 560 to 475 B.C. and was the first poet after Sappho to make love the main theme of his poetry. The subjects of his love poetry were men as well as women, so that Anacreon was the first poet to celebrate homosexuality. In the Roman period he and Sappho became the epitome of romantic poets and were the favorites of young people for hundreds of years. A large following of imitators of Anacreon produced a body of tender, erotic homosexual love poems called *Anacreontea*. According to tradition, Anacreon lived in the court of Polycrates, the ruler of the island of Samos, who also according to tradition kept a coterie of boys around him at all times. Many of Anacreon's poems were addressed to these youths. With the popularity of his poetry, particularly following his death, he was indirectly instrumental in changing much of Classical mythology to fit an outlook less heterosexual than it had had in the days of Homer's Mycenae.[6] A flood of homosexual writings from philosophy to lyric poetry under the indirect influence of Anacreon appeared during the Classical Greek, Hellenistic, and Roman periods. As occurred with the concept of Platonic love when it made its reappearance in Western Europe centuries later, the homosexual tone of Anacreon's poetry was lost or avoided.

In the first odes of Meléndez the reader is immediately aware of a delirious happiness and abandon which paradoxically seem to provide a lurking hint of disaster. Number I, "De mis cantares" ("My Songs"), has the following verses:

After a butterfly,	*(Tras una mariposa,*
Like a simple child	*Cual zagalejo simple,*
Running through the valley,	*Corriendo por el valle,*
I came to lose my way.	*La senda a perder vine.*
I lay down very tired	*Recostéme cansado,*
And such a happy dream	*Y un sueño tan felice*
Assaulted me that, still enjoying it,	*Me asaltó, que aun gozoso*
My lips repeat it.	*Mi labio lo repite.*
Like two youths	*Cual otros dos zagales*
Incredibly handsome,	*De belleza increíble,*
Bacchus and Cupid come	*Baco y Amor se llegan*
To me with light steps;	*A mí con paso libre;*
Cupid, laughing, hurls	*Amor un dulce tiro,*
A love shaft at me,	*Riendo, me despide,*
And on my brow Bacchus	*Y entrambas sienes Baco*
Places a crown of leaves.	*De pámpanos me ciñe.*
They kissed me then;	*Besáronme en la boca*
And thus friendly	*Después; y así apacibles,*

With voices softer	Con voz muy más suave
Than the breeze tell me:	Que el céfiro, me dicen:
"You will never hear the	"Tú de las roncas armas
Terrible sound of harsh arms,	Ni oirás el son terrible,
Nor on a sinking ship	Ni en mal seguro leño
The crashing of rocky shoals.	Bramar las crudas sirtes.
"Peace and love	"La paz y los amores
Will make you, Batilo, famous;	Te harán, Batilo, insigne;
And of Cupid and Bacchus	Y de Cupido y Baco
You will be the gentle swan."	Serás el blando cisne." [7]

The verse form is the same as that in "To My Readers," and provides again a lyrical freedom noted there. The metaphor of the "swan" is intriguing when we remember that it was the preferred image of the Modernists. The exuberance of the poet's feeling is noticeable because of the subject matter—the emotional outpouring of a carefree youth caught by Cupid's shafts and Bacchus' intoxication. The headiness and reckless abandon of this poem very well establish an ambience that is seen at times throughout Meléndez' poetry.

The spirit of abandon is continued in the second ode, entitled "El amor mariposa" ("Love, A Butterfly"). After describing how Cupid turned himself into a butterfly because all the young maidens fled from his menacing love shafts, Meléndez creates a picture of ecstasy and ebullience unimaginable by the totally Neoclassic poet of his day. He writes: "Oh, how beautiful it is!/ Oh, how free it flies,/ And in the sunlight displays/ The brilliance of its purple and nacre." [8]

The motif of *carpe diem* soon appears in full expression. It goes quite naturally with the sybaritic attitude proclaimed in this type of poetry. The idea of "gathering rosebuds while one may" is native to all literatures and has a long history like that of Anacreontic poetry itself. Ode V, "De la primeravera" ("Spring"), is filled with exhortations to enjoy oneself, to grasp the fleeting pleasures of this world. An attitude of indulgent, self-abandon is achieved that has great reminiscences of Góngora's well-known *Letrilla*, "Ándeme yo caliente, y ríase la gente" ("I shall be happy,/ Come what may"). [9] Meléndez exhorts his friends, after describing the rebirth of spring, to reawaken also and enjoy life's pleasures: "Let us drink,/ And in a pleasing banquet/ Let us celebrate the return/ Of April in full flower." [10]

The exuberance that manifests itself in all these poems has a strange twist in Ode IX, "De un baile" ("A Dance"), where Meléndez describes a particularly lively country dance. One of the girls, Anarda, is given special attention because of her effervescent charm. At the end Meléndez brings in the more serious theme of *beatus ille*, the praise of country over city life, when the reader hardly expects great seriousness. This theme recurs throughout Meléndez' poems and at times is expressed sincerely, but often its use is nothing more than that of a literary device cultivated by most all writers of the period. It is a common theme in Cadalso's writing, for example. Cadalso did long for the tranquility of an idealized countryside. Yet, whenever he was in the country for long periods of time, he never seemed to accept the harsh reality of actual country life. The same is true of Iriarte. Meléndez' own use of the theme is intriguing in this poem because the poem in itself is not at all reflective or meditative as those usually are where the theme appears. It is this quality of restrained abandon that gives the poem so much of its charm. Underneath the gaiety and motion in the description of a young girl dancing, one feels a sense of melancholy and a longing on the writer's part to be totally free from the bonds of the world:

> Happy May now returns
> With her serene days,
> And the games and laughter
> Of love follow her.
> From branch to branch sing
> Gentle, young birds
> Full of the fire
> That swells their breasts [. . . .]
> But look at the delirium
> Of Anarda in her daring
> Agility: How well in it
> She paints her passions! [. . . .]
> Oh, innocent breasts!
> Oh, union! oh, simple peace!
> That flees the cities,
> Only inhabiting the country!
> Ah, reign eternal
> Among us, peaceful daughter
> Of Heaven, accompanied
> By joy and happiness! [11]

The incipient reflective mood that overtakes Meléndez, seemingly by accident in this poem, finds expression more at length in other odes in this same Anacreontic grouping. Number X reflects on the passing of life. The poet was only nineteen years old at this time, as the poem makes clear. The tone and the expression are intriguing in their announcement of the early poetry of our twentieth-century Antonio Machado wherein the same ethereal fragility is often projected. Meléndez' poem is entitled "De las riquezas" ("On Wealth"). Its subject is more specific than is Machado's in "Húmedo está bajo el laurel . . ." ("It is damp beneath the laurel tree . . ."), but its questioning lament at the passing of time and youthful illusions strikes the same chord in the reader as do the ending verses of Machado's poem: "¿Será cierto que os vais, sombras gentiles,/ Huyendo entre los árboles de oro?" ("Is it certain that you have gone, O, gentle shadows,/ Fleeing among the golden trees?").[12] Meléndez begins his own poem by saying:

> Now of my early years
> As in a happy dream
> Nineteen have flown
> Without knowing where.
> I call upon them afflicted;
> But I cannot stop them,
> For they flee faster and faster
> No matter how much I entreat them [. . . .] [13]

In Ode XI, "A un ruiseñor" ("To a Nightingale"), Meléndez' reflective attitude becomes even more noticeable. After describing the love of two nightingales and how the male gives expresson to his love through beautiful singing, Meléndez establishes a more personal outlook by wishing he might express his feelings as the bird does. Keats' "Ode to a Nightingale" immediately comes to mind. The use of the nightingale as a symbol of escape, quite early in Meléndez' case, is the same in both poems. Meléndez is not quite so life-weary and tragic in his tone as is the later English Romantic. He feels a certain disgust with the world he lives in, nevertheless, emphasizing it in the last strophe:

> Oh, do not cease
> Your sweet task,

> For my spirit drowns
> In delight at hearing you.
> Thus, let heaven defend
> Your nest from snares,
> And your consort
> Be faithful to you forever.
> I also am a captive:
> I also, if I had
> Your agreeable voice,
> Would tell you my troubles.
> And in simple conversations,
> Exchanging words,
> You would sing your glories,
> And I my simple faith;
> For evil men
> Mock innocence
> And he who tells them his happiness
> Is exposed to their ridicule.[14]

In number XXVII of the *Anacreontic Odes,* "De las ciencias" ("On Science"), included in the 1785 edition and written before September, 1784, the poet appears to react against some of the more meditative attitudes seen so far. The mixture of exuberance and reflection is important in this division of his poetry, just as it is in the entire collection, because it reminds us of the youth and the expected volatility of the poet. Ode XXVII is therefore intriguing in its early autobiographical detail. It tells of Meléndez' education, his turn to the sciences, and the abrupt feeling of desolation they caused. Such self-revelation is ironic when we remember that in the late 1780's the poet turned even more to the realistic, scientific world when he entered the legal field with all its problems and polemics. The refusal in this poem to take life seriously is a poignant testimony by the poet, young at this time, still trying to escape the too great harshness of the world:

> I applied myself to the sciences,
> Thinking in their truths
> To find an easy remedy
> For all my ills.
> Oh, what a silly illusion!
> Oh, how dearly it cost me!
> To my verses I return,

And to my games and dances [. . . .]
Those who study suffer
A thousand troubles and illnesses,
Sleepless and sad,
Silent and serious.
And what do they get? a thousand doubts;
And from these then are born
Other new anxieties
Which bring them more doubts.
Thus they pass their life—
A truly enviable life!—
In arguments and hatreds
Without ever agreeing.
Then, bring me wine, my shepherd girl;
For as long as I have it,
Do not fear that
My happy songs will cease.[15]

As if to emphasize his defiant, mischievous attitude, the poet follows this poem in both the 1785 and *BAE* editions with a short, lascivious ode entitled "Dorila." The whole poem, playful and musical in structure and tone, centers around the deflowering of a young girl. Naturally, plays on the word *flower* are important. The poem is as follows:

To the meadow for flowers
Went young Dorila,
Happy as May,
Pretty as the graces.
She returned home crying,
Upset and pensive,
Her hair disheveled
And her color gone.
They ask her what's wrong,
And she cries out forlorn;
They speak to her, but she does not respond;
They scold her, but she does not reply.
Well, then, what is her illness?
All signs indicate
That when she went for flowers,
She lost the one she had.[16]

Ode XXV, "De mis deseos" ("My Desires"), is the poem that best sums up the poet's feelings while writing these *Anacreontic*

"Light" Poetry of Meléndez

Odes. He addresses Apollo, asking him what is a poet seeking when he drinks and sings. It is certainly not wealth, he for one is sure. He has no desire to envy or to be envied. And to emphasize his attitude he resorts at the end to the *beatus-ille* theme very personally and forthrightly. Indeed, Meléndez sounds uncannily like Fray Luis de León in his "La vida retirada" ("The Peaceful Life"). Whether he will always feel as he does here is irrelevant. He has caught and sealed forever his basic desire for privacy and tranquility. The candid expression of this desire is what attracts us to the poem and creates an empathy between us, the readers, and the poet:

For I, in my poor state,	*(Que yo, en mi pobre estado,*
And in my humble simplicity,	*Y en mi llaneza humilde,*
With a little am content,	*Con poco estoy contento,*
Since with a little one can live.	*Pues con poco se vive.*
And thus I beg you [Apollo] only	*Y así te ruego sólo*
That in peaceful quiet	*Que en quietud apacible*
Innocent and happy	*Inocentes y ledos*
My years may pass by;	*Mis años se deslicen;*
Without my fearing anyone,	*Sin que a ninguno tema,*
Nor for another's state shall I sigh,	*Ni ajeno bien suspire,*
Nor shall my old age	*Ni la vejez cansada*
Be deprived of the pleasures of my lyre.	*De mi lira me prive.)* [17]

There are more *Anacreontic Odes* than I have noted here, some have titles as a group like "La inconstancia: Odas a Lisi" ("Inconstancy: Odes to Lisi") or "La paloma de Filis" ("The Dove of Filis"). These poems have for the most part the effervescent mood we have already seen. The love they exalt or bewail is that of a young man for his beloved who has either reciprocated or spurned his advances. I do not believe that we should consider all the loves that Meléndez presents in his poetry as having occurred in real life. Much of what he wrote, especially in this early love poetry, was a kind of youthful projection or fantasizing carried out in poetic meter. The more earthy aspect of this mental meandering comes out in the poem "Dorila" which we noted above. It comes out elsewhere, most notably in a group of poems called "Los besos de amor" ("The Kisses of Love") published in the late nineteenth century by Raymond Foulché-Delbosc.

Foulché discovered these poems along with some by Iriarte and Leandro Fernández de Moratín and others. He was impressed especially by Meléndez' odes and believed they were written about 1780. They all deal with the more physical aspects of love, although in general their tone is not too different from that of the *Anacreontic Odes* we have seen so far, only a little more realistic in detail. They are quite similar to some licentious, earthy poems by Samaniego, Iriarte, *et al*, also published by Foulché in a collection called *Cuentos y poesías más que picantes* (*Stories and Poems More Than Racy*). All this poetry indicates that the poets were quite capable of using the pastoral mode to depict a real world when they wanted. The more earthy attitude of this particular poetry has its parallels in the earthy side of the courtly-love lyrics of the Middle Ages. With Meléndez and the other poets here, we have simply an eighteenth-century manifestation of the same attitude.

Foulché published twenty-three of Meléndez' odes which he entitled *The Kisses of Love*. Several of the odes are much more graphic than the random selections quoted below, but these nevertheless give some idea as to what the poems contain:

> When I rest on your sweet lips,
> My beloved,
> Sucking in the fragrant flowers
> Of your breath,
> One of the Gods
> That dwell on Olympus
> I believe myself, and more,
> If a more glorious fortune there can be.

> ❋ ❋ ❋ ❋ ❋ ❋ ❋

> O beautiful quarrels!
> O soft bites!
> Do you wish, Nisa, to make me
> Happy? then, always deny
> Me your kisses
> So I can thus
> Enjoy them, softly
> Stolen from your mouth.

> ❋ ❋ ❋ ❋ ❋ ❋ ❋

Amorous dove,
Enough; do not complain,
For already
I cling to you;
Already my sweet mouth
Drinks from yours
Your breath sweeter
Than sweet honey;
My tongue wanders,
My breast burns within,
Oh, I die in love! [18]

After the *Anacreontic Odes* in the *BAE* edition come the *letrillas*, poems by Meléndez which are extremely musical and pleasant to the ear. In their mocking playfulness they again remind the reader of certain poems of Góngora. The tone of "Ándeme yo caliente . . ." is again achieved in *Letrilla* XV, "En un convite de amistad" ("At a Party of Friends"), whose refrain is "Let us drink/ Of the soft liquor,/ Singing drunkenly/ To Bacchus, and not to love." Number XVI, "El vino y la amistad suavizan los más graves trabajos" ("Wine and Friendship Lighten the Most Serious Hardships"), is similar: "To the winds our troubles:/ Fill the glasses;/ For wine and friendship/ Sweeten everything." [19]

Letrilla XIV, "La despedida" ("The Farewell"), contains a certain youthful freedom and independence in its spirit. The poet is bidding farewell to his beloved Filis. The seemingly profound emotion at the moment of separation recalls similar expression in Garcilaso and announces the languid bitterness of Bécquer. The first strophe, a beautiful expression of farewell, portrays a sadness and melancholy, both enhanced by a slow musical beat, that also announce a specific passage from Byron. He too could be truly personal when he wanted, as at the imminent separation from his wife: "Fare thee well! and if for ever/ Still for ever, fare thee well [. . . .]" [20] Meléndez' emotion is hardly different: "Farewell, my sweet life,/ Filis, farewell; for Fate/ My end has decreed,/ And I must leave." [21] The poem's lingering sense of fragility and farewell is important. It reemphasizes the fact that the supposed lighter poetry does have depth to it when one looks for it. In this instance, the depth lies in the evocative expression.

A group of idylls follows the *letrillas*, and in them an essentially bucolic, pastoral ambience is achieved. Number II, "La corderita" ("The Little Lamb"), is a good example of the airy, musical quality of these poems. It starts off in a sort of singsong fashion: "My little lamb,/ Today I want to take you/ To my Filis/ In feudal homage." [22]

Idyll III, "La ausencia" ("Absence"), is interesting for its use of nature as a universal mirror, the "pathetic fallacy" so aptly designated later by Ruskin. Filis is here the subject who laments the absence of her beloved: "Today everything has changed:/ The force of the heat/ Withers the valleys,/ And dries up the streams." [23] The poem is full of the diminutive endings (*clavellinas, cuitadilla*, etc.) so beloved by Meléndez. The narration from the girl's standpoint is unusual and for this reason intriguing. Meléndez had acute psychological understanding of the frustrated and forlorn, male or female. When Filis addresses nature, her outcry is not artificial. Even though she uses the poetic device of the universal mirror, she manages to convey a sense of real pathos and anguish. Meléndez' achievement in her creation is therefore even more an indication of his artistic abilities.

One of the idylls is a translation from Theocritus. I include Meléndez' version of the poem because its tone is rather different from that of the poems seen so far. It is earthy and lascivious, in the vein of some in the *Kisses of Love*. Even though it is not an original work, Meléndez' treatment of it is his own. It points out well that the poet did not really have his mind lost in some artificial world of vaporous creatures. The pastoral scene evoked with amusing brashness in the four verses below emphasizes what the pastoral world was actually like. The shepherdess replies to the shepherd's attempts at lovemaking in a realistic but degrading fashion: " 'What a nice beard you have, and so much/ Hair! your lips are those of a sick man,/ Your hands are black, and you even smell bad./ Get away from me, and do not contaminate me.' " [24]

The grouping of *romances* or ballads in the *BAE* volume is varied in content. Many are very light in tone and exhibit the exuberance and freshness of the early odes. Others are more restrained and impart glimpses of the mentality that produced them, troubled or perplexed for some particular reason at the moment. One of the most beautiful in expression is number XV, "Los segadores" ("The Harvesters"). The poem is fairly long, beginning and ending with the same four-line stanza. The regularity of the meter enhances the settled, calm ambience. The scene begs comparison to the early nineteenth-century painting *The Cornfield* by the English artist John Constable. The same fragile, ethereal beauty that that painting evokes is here in Meléndez' poem. In essence, the poem is a praise of country life personalized in an old man who talks of nature and of God who has put order in His universe for the good of all His creatures. Essentially, he exhorts his fellowmen to go out and work the fields of man's Benefactor: "Thus we imitate the good Lord,/ Who gives to us with open hands;/ To open ours is to thank Him,/ And to close them, to anger Him." The picture is one of total peace and harmony at the end, again reminding us of the Constable painting with its almost impressionistic stream flowing into the vague distance. Plácido, the old man, finishes his paternalistic speech, and he and his followers go off to the fields in the young, spring morning:

> In Plácido's face
> The innocence of his soul
> And respect shine imprisoned
> In his venerable locks.
> Raising the curved sickles
> With noisy tumult,
> All followed the old man,
> And he happy kept calling to them:
> "Reapers, to the harvest;
> For already the young morning
> Opens her rosy doors
> To the Sun who rises in the East." [25]

Perhaps better than any one other grouping of poems, the ballads show Meléndez' Romantic spirit beginning to surface. Nature, increasingly more forceful, even violent, appears in these poems with great regularity. This is due to the poet's inherent love for the outside world, for nature in her primeval and pristine state. From a more formal, rigid presentation in the form and attitude of nature in some of his other poems, Meléndez goes to a freer, more exuberant attitude in the *romances*. This shift in literary emphasis has a close parallel in the changing appearance of nature in eighteenth-century gardens. Gardens of the earlier portion of the century are well represented in our own country at the Governor's Palace in Williamsburg, Virginia. Laid out in strict geometrical form in the mid-1700's, the garden has a fascinating section called a maze. This labyrinthine construction built to confound the illogical visitor is indicative of both Neoclassic and Romantic minds working at the same time. In its demand for a precise, logical personality to wend its paths successfully, the maze represents the precision of Neoclassicism. In its hint of chaos and the overwhelming power of nature in its control of man, it is Romantic in intent. The final stamp is purely Neoclassic, however. Overlooking the maze is a small mount on which are benches for the viewer to sit and watch the travails of the lost wanderers below. The satirical side of Neoclassicism thus comes out beautifully in one of the best examples of eighteenth-century landscaping in this country.

The gardens of the later eighteenth century lost much of their rigidity and formality. Their creators at times went to the opposite extreme of their predecessors and created an artificial wilderness by hauling in boulders and other nonnative material to produce a more "natural" effect. Two of Meléndez' *romances* show this same new treatment of nature in literature. Besides pointing up the Romantic side of Meléndez, these ballads have the added attraction of showing how the arts in any one period can have a close correlation.

The first of these poems is ballad XXIX, "La mañana" ("Morning"). It is an impressionistic, delicate painting of morning. Nature, most evident throughout the poem, is not presented in her wild, forceful manner at this point because Meléndez, the obvious Romantic on these occasions, is attempting rather to portray her here in all her innocence and candor. Morning's approach is measured and ethereal in the first strophe as Meléndez calls upon the birds to sing at her arrival. The image that is immediately suggested is like one of those fair, but ever-so-distant women portrayed by the pre-Raphaelite artists in the mid-nineteenth century: "Leave your nests, little birds,/ And with a thousand happy songs/ Greet the new day/ That approaches from the East." [26] The poet himself is placed in an ecstasy of joy at her approach. In the fourth strophe he bursts into rapturous exclamations and achieves in words what the painter's brush would on canvas: "Oh, the clouds of dawn!/ With what bursts

of brilliance/ They are lighted,/ And enriched with gold!" [27]
The spectator of the celestial change of night to day finds his
own emotions changing also. From a sad, pensive person he
becomes a happy, lighthearted one. A reverse sort of universal
mirror or pathetic fallacy, a more healthy one, is at work: "Everything comes out from dreams/ With her and is refreshed,/ As if
this day/ Were the happy dawn of the world." [28] As morning's
approach progresses, the entire world is turned into a place of
confused, delirious happiness. Nothing escapes this change that
slowly overtakes all in its path.

The contrast of images is startling, and it is not until the
end that the poet uses a personal pronoun for himself and calls
his beloved out to experience the voluptuous rapture that so
enchantingly has arrived. The development of the poet's thought
can be seen in the following verses:

> This tumult, this joy
> Which universally antecedes
> The singing of the hymn to the day
> Reanimating all living beings;
> This delirium of voices
> Which in its frenzy deafens—
> So many birds' songs,
> So many fervent hymns;
> This inexplicable fervor,
> This boiling movement
> In ineffable delight
> Of an infinity of birds,
> From the humble blade of grass
> To the most eminent oak,
> From the insect to the daring bird
> Which tries to fly to the sun;
> Oh, how it all enchants me! Oh, how
> My breast beats and burns,
> And in the general happiness
> Becomes crazy with joy! [. . . .]
> How beautiful is, Silvia,
> The morning! how much it has
> To admire! in its beauty
> How my soul is moved!
> Leave your bed, and come to the country,
> That happily offers you

Its aroma and flowers, and together
Let us enjoy so many pleasures.[29]

The last verses above are amusing in a way. Even with all the
early Romantic tone of the rest of the poem, Meléndez is still
not free of the poetic devices of the other side of his inspiration.
The pastoral, airy world of shepherdesses and shepherds appears
in the mere addressing of Silvia. The call to enjoy the pleasures
brought by morning only more forcefully reminds us of the
importance of that pastoral world in Meléndez' creative processes.
    One other ballad is important in its portrayal of nature and
shows a rather early, full-blown Romantic spirit. The ballad is
actually two combined under the title of "Doña Elvira." In their
tone the poems are an antecedent of the historical ballads or
leyendas cultivated in the early nineteenth century by the Duke
of Rivas. Meléndez' poems interest us here especially in their
creation of ambience. At the beginning of the first ballad, nature
is pictured at her most violent and destructive. The lines are a
good example of the typical nineteenth-century Romantic's pleasure in the threat of destruction and doom. Nature, we are to
understand, is indeed the harbinger of fatal and dire events. We
must keep in mind, however, that this extraordinary, wild vision
of Meléndez alternates with that more delicate, seductive one in
"Morning." The next lines from "Doña Elvira" are indicative of
only one facet of his inspiration—the melancholy, lugubrious,
freedom-loving one:

> I do not know what grave misfortune
> The heavens predict to me
> For they seem toppled
> From their eternal poles.
> All bloodied the moon
> Does not shine; it frightens the earth,
> When darkness does not swallow up
> Its faint reflections.
> In a horrible war
> Emboldened the winds fight,
> Their shrill cry filling
> My frozen breast with fear.
> The leafy forest roars,
> And it seems that there far off,

> Carried on the clouds,
> A thousand lugubrious beings moan.[30]

There are other divisions of Meléndez' poetry—*sonetos, silvas, elegías, epístolas, discursos,* etc. They all contain evidences of the so-called lighter vein of his thought as well as more profoundly philosophical and political expression. Contrary to some critics' affirmations, we must emphasize that it is impossible to divide Meléndez' poetry conveniently into two catagories—one, a light poetry that abruptly becomes a second more philosophical outpouring after Jovellanos' influence is stronger. As in the poetry we have seen so far, Meléndez' attitudes cover a wide spectrum, from high effervescence to deep melancholy. The small group of sonnets reminds us of this fact immediately. The variety of emotions that Meléndez achieves in this rigid poetic form is astonishing. The first one (number one in the 1785 edition also), entitled "El despecho" ("Despair"), is filled with a Romantic melancholy that colors the entire world for him in sorrowful shades because of the emptiness he feels. The loss of the beloved's favor causes him to find no solace anywhere:

> I flee to solitude, and with me
> Goes hidden my sorrow, and nothing amuses me;
> In the city I drown in tears;
> I abhor my being; and although I curse
> Life, I fear that death may even be
> A weak solace for such misery.[31]

The pessimism in the above poem is forgotten in another, Number XIV (XI in the 1785 edition), "El ruego encarecido" ("The Insistent Entreaty"). Here a frivolity and abandon are presented not unlike the atmosphere noted at more length when we considered the *Anacreontic Odes.* The freshness and exuberance of this sonnet captivate the reader and present Meléndez to him in his sunniest disposition:

> Leave your hut now, my shepherdess;
> Leave it, my beloved;
> Come, for already in the East the day is dawning,
> And the sun gilds the peaks of the mountains.
> Come, and to the humble breast that adores you,

Return happiness with your presence.
Oh, if you delay, my soul will distrust;
Oh, come, and alleviate my pain, my love.
A garland woven of a thousand flowers
And a fragrant, delicate rose
I have for you, Filis, when you come.
I shall give them to you singing my love,
I shall give them to you, my sweet; and you loving
Will give me a luscious kiss.[32]

IV *Painting and Poetry*

At several points in this chapter we have noted the similarities
of Meléndez' poetry to literary works both before and after his
time. Certain resemblances in mood and tone of his poetry to
that found in some artistic schools and individual artists have
also been pointed out. There was a purpose behind such comparisons. In this final section of the chapter, in more detailed
comparisons this time between certain poems by Meléndez and
certain paintings of an eighteenth-century artist, we shall see
that Meléndez did indeed follow artistic criteria of his time.
There is a tremendous need to comprehend Meléndez and his
artistic criteria from his own viewpoint. The late nineteenth and
early twentieth centuries in European painting, music, and poetry
provide a striking example of the correlations among the arts. One
can "hear" Monet's painting in the music of Debussy. And in
Spanish literature one can "read" both painting and music in the
early poetry of Antonio Machado. The relationship between
eighteenth-century painting and poetry may not be quite so
obvious at first glance, but this should not prevent our attempting to establish a close connection.

Essentially the world of Rococo is what we encounter in
Meléndez' poetry. This artistic movement, later joined to the
Baroque in the mind of the Neoclassicist, was evident in the first
half of the eighteenth century all over Europe. To a lesser extent
it was notable in England, although Chippendale furniture with
its Oriental motif was surely an outgrowth of the Rococo spirit.
The origin of the term is the French *rocaille*, meaning *rock-work*,
rockery. Rocks were first used in the decoration of gardens in
France in the sixteenth century. Small glittering rocks and shells
to encrust grottoes and to heighten the effects of fountains often
created a brilliant scene of airiness and grace. *Rocaille* as a term

was soon applied to an ornamental style developed in France at the beginning of the eighteenth century that first appeared in interior design and then spread to other areas. Basic to this artistic concept was the development of the line—which was twisted into curves, shells, and scrolls, and applied on surfaces like mirrors or porcelain. All sorts of exuberant, seemingly asymmetrical motifs resulted. In this characteristic, Rococo approximated the convolutions of the Baroque style. Against such emotional manifestations, it was only natural that the Neoclassic school would later react. The Rococo, the *modern style*, as it soon came to be called, quickly spread in popularity from about 1700 on.

During the regency of Philip of Orléans, and then under the able protection of Louis XV's mistress and adviser, Mme. de Pompadour, the three most outstanding representatives of this artistic school flourished. They were Antoine Watteau (1684–1721), François Boucher (1703–1770), and Jean Honoré Fragonard (1732–1806). Watteau specifically personified the deeply refined spirit of the age. Fragonard and Boucher, the latter the artistic favorite of Mme. de Pompadour, created a lyrical, exuberant, sensual world of mythology, and transported it into the salons. The vigorous creative activity of these three artists and others changed taste fantastically in the arts. Most later reaction to the movement was against its supposed superficiality, yet the Rococo may be considered a further outpouring of the wild, abandoned emotion of the Baroque at the loss of a central core of control, its faith in God. The Neoclassicist could not accept the Baroque-Rococo artist's despair, but even in the heyday itself of Rococo the style was much criticized.

The Rococo spirit flourished, then, in the first half of the century, yet only under severe attack. Whether or not we accept that originally, inherently, there was a spiritual anguish propelling this artistic movement forward, on the surface it did undoubtedly express a deep craving for a pleasant world of dreams. Between the Rococo's seeming frivolity and the more subdued effect of Neoclassical art, it would seem hard to find a bridge. Nevertheless, a link does appear in the art of Rococo's greatest exponent, Antoine Watteau. While his art is very much an outgrowth of his time, it has a personal feeling lacking in the works of some of his contemporaries. For our purposes it is Watteau's style that most easily provides a comparison to Meléndez' "lighter" poetry. One art critic notes Watteau's similarity to Mozart in "his combination of profundity with artifice, and the quiet melancholy that seems to suffuse his scenes of happiness." [33] A similar comparison can be made regarding the poetry of Meléndez and the painting of Watteau. Such a comparison further develops the idea of the correspondence among the arts in the eighteenth century and also happily underscores our earlier reference to synesthesia. Pastoral poetry therefore, with its great emphasis on love and its joys or tribulations, the Anacreontic mode, that is, has a natural counterpart in Rococo painting. The depiction on canvas of country scenes with aristocratic figures in shepherd dress expresses the same longing for escape that verses depicting these scenes express on paper.

Watteau made a particular contribution to the pastoral scene, the *fête champêtre*. Such a painting is an idealized portrayal of nature peopled with figures ordinarily in contemporary dress. By making a brief comparison of the ambience in one of Watteau's paintings and in Meléndez' first and most famous eclogue, "Batilo," we can begin to see the relationship of the poet's work to that of Watteau and to the Rococo sensibility in general.

Meléndez' "Batilo" is a dialogue among three personages— Batilo, Arcadio, and the Poet. The poem has a subtitle of significance in our comparison, "En alabanza de la vida del campo" ("In Praise of Country Life"). That is, the theme of *beatus ille* is the principal one. We find on beginning to read the poem that this is not a picture of pure country life, of real shepherds and farmers, but of that always idealized life so natural to this theme. Batilo begins the poem with an exhortation to his sheep to graze and enjoy the beginning of a new day. Arcadio soon comes on the scene, praising the beauty of nature. The two shepherds converse, continuing to praise nature, and recalling remarks made on other occasions by their friends Elpino, Delio, and Dalmiro— who in real life were Llaguno, Diego González, and Cadalso. All on one occasion or another had reacted against a life full of turmoil and upheaval. Dalmiro had told them of the horrors of the sea which he had seen on his way to war:

> And Dalmiro would tell,
> He who went to war
> And saw the lands where day dies,

> How the river of this mountain range
> In no way resembled
> The mighty sea, which caused him fear.[34]

The poem is not at all lacking in an essential lyricism. In one of Batilo's lengthy utterances, the shepherd breaks forth into a series of lyrical declarations that again recall Fray Luis and announce Antonio Machado:

> Oh, glorious solitude!
> Oh, valley! oh, dark forest!
> Oh, tangled jungle! oh, pure fountain!
> Oh, fortunate life!
> Oh, serene, clear river,
> Who run softly by the willow trees! [35]

In this same section, Meléndez, through Batilo, notes how the wealthy city dwellers come out to enjoy the beauties he has just been describing. His attitude is rather extraordinary here because in real life Meléndez was one of those city dwellers himself. The poet is both within and without his poem at this point. He exists in his poem very much as Watteau does in his figures superimposed on the idealized natural scenes of his paintings:

> And surely, how many times
> Do the greatest lords
> Come to our poor huts
> Without pomp or haughtiness,
> To enjoy the favors
> Of the country and its simple pleasures? [36]

Meléndez speaks more forthrightly at the end in the personage of the Poet. We easily see his longing to escape to the world he has fabricated. While that world in our eyes may be too contrived, even ridiculous, to the Poet it is a creation of his imagination wherein he really can escape the rigors of an everyday life he finds too burdensome. At this point we are encountering an anguish or *Angst* that exists within the actual structure of the poem:

> Thus went praising
> Their innocent life
> The two enamored shepherds [. . .]
> And I, who overheard them

Behind a leafy beech tree,
Comparing my life to theirs,
Cursed my state.
From then on the city vexed me,
And a thousand happy days
I enjoyed in their fortunate abodes.[37]

Of the various paintings by Watteau that might be the setting
for the above scene, there is one that captures the basic ambience
quite well. It is *Le Rendez-vous De Chasse* (*The Halt During
the Hunt*) now in the Wallace Collection in London. It is an
enormous canvas with an illusion of even greater size because of
its broad perspective. In the distance the viewer sees a tremendous
glow of light from the sun that recalls some of Claude Lorrain's
more spectacular visions. In the mid-distance, and silhouetted
against the light, is a small group of figures. A surrounding leafy
forest makes them stand out and also draws them together in a
symmetrical whole with the distant view and a larger group of
figures in the immediate foreground. The latter figures include
men and women (who hardly seem dressed for a hunt) and
several horses and dogs. The atmosphere imbued with a quality
of innocence is one of restrained elegance. The natural setting
itself intimates delicateness, tenderness, and evanescence. A sort
of ethereal melancholy, emphasized by the idealized picture of
nature, permeates the scene.

The similarities of the poem "Batilo" and the painting *Le
Rendez-vous* can be reduced to two essential ones with the figures
in both the poem and the painting serving as the key. First, in
the poem the pastoral names for Meléndez' contemporaries are
the result of the same artistic criterion that caused the figures to
be placed in the painting. The poet and the artist have imposed a
real world on a romanticized, imagined one. Second, the poses
of the figures in the painting reflect the expounding of the *beatus-
ille* theme in the poem. This theme is not a call to the real world
of country life, but to a stylized one. This in no way reduces that
life's charm, of course, but rather enhances it. Intent and portrayal
in both works of art are the same, therefore. And the poet's
attempt to become a part of his fiction at the end of his poem
is no different from the artist's efforts to enforce elegant figures
on an idealized backdrop. The surprising thing about each work

is that neither really seems false or artificial if we see them as products of the age-old longing for escape. By no means is such a desire ever inherently superficial.

Two other paintings of Watteau seem to announce the scene that Meléndez creates in a ballad, Number XXXIV, "La tarde" ("Afternoon"). One of the paintings, a good example of a *fête champêtre*, is called *Assemblée Dans Un Parc* (*Group in a Park*) and is now in the Louvre. The painting is a marvelous portrayal of nature. With its impressionistic verdure and gold, hazy tone in the distance, it early announces the ambience of some of Constable's most beautiful paintings years later. In the foreground is once again a small group of elegantly dressed people. They give the impression of watching the beauty of nature just as we are doing outside the picture. For this reason, and because of the almost excessive effeteness they project, they do seem a little artificial to us. In fact, it is thought that the figures were super-imposed later by Watteau on the natural scene. The other paint-ing, also in the Louvre, is perhaps Watteau's best known, *L'Embarquement Pour L'île De Cythère* (*The Embarkation for Cythera*). It was painted in 1717 and presents a group of lovers, neatly paired off, returning from the Isle of Love after having made votive offerings to Venus. The tranquil scene is bathed in the golden light of afternoon. Mountainous crags are seen in the distance, ominous yet softened by the gold and copper tones of evening. In the near distance several cherubs or cupids fly about with banners. A Venus herm is in the right foreground, aloofly smiling at her powers. What most intrigues us is the almost melancholy lighting, heightened by the way it plays on the figures in the foreground and on the natural scene in the distance. There is another painting of this theme, but it lacks the inherent sadness that draws us to make a comparison of this first painting to Meléndez' poem.

Meléndez' "Afternoon" is in many ways a verbal painting. Its underlying tone is personal, longing and melancholy, but with enough restraint to prevent its being totally Romantic. It antici-pates that movement, however, just as the ambience of the two paintings noted above does. Time in the poem is late afternoon as the sun sets. The tone of elegance provided by the personages in the paintings is provided by the elegance of the vocabulary in the poem. The description of the close of day in the first lines is a good example. I include the Spanish so we may see more fully the tone of this particular poem: "Now delightful Hesperus,/ Among peaceful the clouds,/ As the precursor of night,/ Comes out of the West." (*Ya el Héspero delicioso,/ Entre nubes agradables,/ Cual precursor de la noche,/ Por el Occidente sale.*)[38]

The poet is overwhelmed by the beauty that surrounds him. He first definitively enters his poetic recreation of this beauty in a series of exclamations: "Oh, such shades! such colors!/ Such brilliant clouds/ My eyes intoxicated/ See everywhere!" (*¡Oh! ¡qué visos! ¡que colores!/ ¡Que ráfagas tan brillantes/ Mis ojos embebecidos/ Registran de todas partes!*) He is soon led to more philosophical reflections:

It seems the universe,	*(El universo parece*
Tired from its incessant action,	*Que, de su acción incesante*
Desires rest,	*Cansado, el reposo anhela,*
And is going to abandon itself to sleep.	*Y al sueño va a abandonarse.*
Everything is peace, silence,	*Todo es paz, silencio todo,*
Everything in these solitudes	*Todo en estas soledades*
Moves me, and makes bearable	*Me conmueve, y hace dulce*
The memory of my misfortunes.	*La memoria de mis males.)*[39]

It is no accident that the fifth verse of this quotation sounds like the beginning of Don Quixote's description of his own idealized Golden Age. The poet, lulled into a kind of quixotically idealized state, has become one with the universe. He abandons himself totally to this new world: "I abandon myself to its impulse." But he soon becomes too lost in this world and feels anxiety. Nature, her powers seductively but ominously cloaked in the paintings, begins to menace the artist here in the poem. The feeling is the same as in the painting *Embarkation* where the distant crags softly threaten. Meléndez carries the threat further and develops a feeling of nature's potential throughout the poem. He becomes unable to control his rising terror, a terror that interestingly exists in the new, supposedly peaceful world he is creating: "My steps hurry on;/ But nothing helps my fear,/ For the gigantic shadows/ Follow, terrifying." (*Mis pasos se precipitan;/Mas nada en mi alivio vale,/ Que agigantadas las sombras/ Me siguen para aterrarle.*) The incipient terror is perversely attractive, however, and he soon desires what just before seemed most ominous to him: "Fleeing, I cross the moun-tain-top,/ And on seeing its savage peaks,/ 'Oh,' I exclaim, 'that I could like them/ Become insensitive.'" (*Trepo, huyéndolas, la cima,/ Y al ver sus riscos salvajes,/ "¡Ay!" exclamo, "¡quién, cual ellos,/ Insensible se tornase!"*) He ends his soliloquy with a kind of summation:

Thus disturbed and fearful	*(Así, azorado y medroso,*
I begin to complain to heaven	*Al cielo empiezo a quejarme*
Of my bitter misfortunes,	*De mis amargas desdichas,*
And to cry out painfully;	*Y a lanzar dolientes ayes;*
While the last moment expires	*Mientras de la luz dudosa*
Of the hesitant light,	*Espira el último instante,*
And night spreads its mantle,	*Y el manto la noche tiende,*
That destroys the dusk.	*Que el crepúsculo deshace.)* [40]

This portrayal of nature is almost a Romantic one, but the feeling of restraint is still too strong. We do not see here that wild, ferocious nature noted earlier in the two ballads of "Doña Elvira." We have basically a Rococo atmosphere which the poet's personality cannot directly enter. Nature provides both a refuge and a Hell for him, Meléndez implies. The same is true of Watteau in his paintings. Profound feelings of nostalgia, melancholy, and isolation are conveyed in his representation of the natural scene. Just as Meléndez holds back from a total abandonment to his creation, noted above in his vocabulary, for example, Watteau infuses his paintings with an elegant restraint personified in his figures. In Watteau's *Group in the Park*, the figures make us hesitate before entering the wilder, more Romantic world behind them. In his *Embarkation*, the figures are more real in their seeming expression of emotion, but they nevertheless, in all their finery, again prevent our losing ourselves in the idealized world in the distance.

The flamboyant effusiveness of Rococo art eventually gave way to the more rigid criteria of Neoclassicism. In Spain, the painting of the Neoclassic artist Raphael Mengs (to whom Meléndez refers specifically in his Ode XIX, read before the Academy of St. Ferdinand in 1787) was receiving royal favor before Meléndez ever began writing. But it would be the very

JUAN MELÉNDEZ VALDÉS

end of the century before Jacques Louis David would make the
Neoclassic manifesto in art definitive. Painting in the eighteenth
century was quite varied, therefore. This variety was heightened,
too, by the fact that the arts did not develop together in strictly
chronological fashion. In his earliest poetry, Meléndez followed
essentially the dictates of a school of art, the Rococo, which by
1750 was beginning to pass out of vogue. Even more important,
tones of that school permeate all his poetry, mingling with new
Romantic inspirations.

In conclusion then, Meléndez' poetry, even when the astonishing quantity of it makes critics think differently at times, is not
really artificial. It only appears that way if we do not understand
the artistic credo the poet was following, especially in the beginning of his literary career. In the tremendous amount of his
poetry Meléndez has left us, there is no one set mood or attitude.
We saw in the examples in this chapter how even within his
"Rococo" poetry, just as in Rococo art, there is great variety of
emotion. To call Meléndez' poetry "light" or "superficial" is thus
highly erroneous.

[86]

CHAPTER 3

Philosophy and Poetry

I Neoclassicism in Spanish Literature

IN the previous chapter, we established that for that so-called "lighter" poetry there were definite artistic criteria at work in Meléndez' mind. Indeed, for all his poetry there were definite artistic and philosophical criteria. It is to understand these that we include this chapter in our study.

In 1797, the same year that the second edition of Meléndez' poetry appeared, the Spanish writer José Mor de Fuentes included a comment in his novel *La Serafina* that shows the admiration and love with which Meléndez was regarded in his day. The remark serves as a point of departure here in our analysis of Meléndez' attitudes and general philosophy: "May the gentle, lyrical, chaste Meléndez live a thousand centuries. Only he in his divine poems knows how to attract and madden innocent hearts with the only truly estimable objects of nature. That is to say, objects like trees, fields of grain, flowers, streams, birds, and flocks of sheep. I only wish that I could make of my Serafina another Rosana, that is (although it may appear contradictory), an adorable country girl." [1]

The novelist appreciates the sunniness, the freedom, the fragility, and above all the personalism to be found in Meléndez' poetry. The surprising openness of his poetry and the emotional impact of his message greatly attracted the first admirers and spread his reputation among all segments of the population. It was this very personalism, as we have pointed out before, that distinguished Meléndez and the school to which he belonged from the more formal Neoclassic writers who were often unable to bridge the gap between literary theory and public popularity.

Besides showing us how great was Meléndez' widespread popularity and easy familiarity with his audience, the above passage hints at various fundamental aesthetic criteria in the poet's work. The question of realism versus idealism presents itself here. We have already established in the previous chapter that what superficially seems frivolous or inconsequential in Meléndez' poetry is actually only the result of an artistic attitude that proposed artificiality to cover up a more profound intent lurking beneath its pretty façade. With the bugaboo of banality removed, we can expect to find in Meléndez' work something far more concrete than initially meets our eye. Exactly what was Meléndez' concept of literary reality, we must ask ourselves as we continue in our investigation of his poetry. The most important thing for us to realize in our study is Meléndez' crucial position as an innovator and, specifically, as a bridge between old and new artistic philosophies.

There is one literary phenomenon we find well personified in Meléndez—the gradual development of the Romantic attitude that occurred in his lifetime. Better than any other Spanish writer, he exemplifies what happened in the ever-changing literary outlook of the century. In many ways the Romantic attitude developed concurrently with the Neoclassic one. The two are not so inimical as we might at first believe. Each developed from and fed off the other. Meléndez Valdés was in a unique position to represent the development of the two movements, especially the Romantic, as they flowered in the latter half of the Spanish eighteenth century. His inherently romantic or escapist point of view made him receptive to philosophical and literary currents and allowed him to mold them to his own manner of thinking. Meléndez manifests a progressive development in Spanish literature of the time contiguous with emerging Romantic tendencies throughout Europe. The Romantic attitude thus begins in Spain long before the appearance of the Zorrillas, the Esproncedas, and other Spanish Romantics of the nineteenth century. Romanticism in Spain even antecedes its appearance elsewhere in one particular way that we shall note at the end of this chapter. This fact cannot be repeated too often when we consider that for the last one hundred and fifty years or so, critics have decried the literature of eighteenth-century Spain, proclaiming somehow a miraculous flowering of Romanticism in the 1830's. That so-called flowering was indeed an outburst, but it was so purely from political, not literary, reasons.

To see how Romanticism might reflect or offset Neoclassicism, it is necessary to look at the basic proposals of the Neoclassic school of literature. It is not in itself an easy task to outline these tenets, for like all philosophies, literary or otherwise, they involve human beings who naturally are quite varied in their own individual attitudes. In Chapter 2 of this book, we briefly referred to Ignacio de Luzán to note that Meléndez was connected with the Neoclassic school early in his life. Meléndez was seen to diverge from the Neoclassic tenets principally through a more personal approach in his poetry.

The Spanish Neoclassic movement in poetry has often been misunderstood since its very origins. If not conceived of as simply an empty French, and therefore essentially political, importation, it was considered by contemporary detractors as too cold in contrast with the remains of the Gongoristic-Conceptistic schools of the previous century. A pertinent synopsis of this somewhat negative attitude comes at the beginning of the nineteenth century. Simonde de Sismondi's *De La Littérature Du Midi De L'Europe* (*The Literature of the South of Europe*), first published in 1813, has a long paragraph on Luzán's significance in Spanish letters. It contains, mildly stated, all the past, contemporary, and future prejudices against Luzán and the movement he formally brought to Spain. The section reads in part:

That party of literary critics who endeavoured to reform the national taste, and adapt it to the French model, had at its head, at the middle of the last century, a man of great talents and extensive information, who had a considerable influence on the character and productions of his contemporaries. This was Ignazio de Luzán, member of the Academies of language, history, and painting, a counsellor of state, and minister of commerce. He was attached to poetry, and himself composed verses with elegance. He found in his nation no trace of criticism, except among the imitators of Gongora, who had reduced to rules all the bad taste of their school. It was for the avowed purpose of attacking these that he carefully studied the principles of Aristotle and those of the French authors; and as he was himself more remarkable for elegance and correctness of style, than for an energetic and fertile imagination, he sought less to unite the French correctness to the eminent qualities of his countrymen, than to introduce a foreign literature in the place of that possessed by the nation. In conformity with these principles, and in order to reform the taste of his country, he composed his celebrated Treatise on Poetry, printed at Saragossa in 1737, in a folio volume of five hundred pages. This work, written with great judgment and a display of vast erudition, clear without languor, elegant and unaffected, was received by men of letters as a masterpiece, and has ever since been cited by the classical party in Spain as containing the basis and rules of true taste. The principles which Luzán lays down with regard to poetry, considered as an [sic] useful and instructive amusement, rather than as a passion of the soul, and an exercise of one of the noblest faculties of our being, are such as have been repeated in all treatises of this kind, until the time when the Germans began to regard this art from a more elevated point of view, and substituted for the poetics of the peripatetic philosopher a more happy and ingenious analysis of the mind and the imagination.[2]

The reluctant reception accorded Spanish Neoclassicism by many Spaniards themselves is well mirrored here in the begrudging recognition of Luzán by one of the earliest French Romantic literary critics. The dependence of Spanish Neoclassicism on French writers is subtly underscored in the quotation as if Luzán's work were merely a rendering in Spanish of their views. In an incisive essay, Russell Sebold has recently shown that French influence on Luzán's *Poetics* actually was very little.[3] The theme of his article also quite conveniently disproves the supposedly great indebtedness of Spanish to French Neoclassicism.

Sebold, in another significant essay, has also noted the true essence of Spanish Neoclassicism. Concluding a study of Tomás de Iriarte, he writes the following opportune lines:

The genius of the *Literary Fables* is only one of the many testimonies that texts offer of the great necessity to reconsider the historiographic and artistic ideas with which we look at Spanish Neoclassic literature. It is useless to insist that the greatest or least merit of the works of that movement must come from the degree of Spanish spirit they exude—as useless as putting a madrigal to the same tests as an epic poem. *Precisely what the Spanish Neoclassicist wished to produce*—as in analogous movements in other countries—*was an unadorned art without frontiers* [italics mine]. Only by remembering this condition is it possible to understand the art of certain writers of the eighteenth century. The fact that such an art was achieved in Spanish must not be seen, as has been the case, as a sin against literary patriotism, but as one more proof of the eternal adaptability of the language of the *Cid* and of the *Romancero* in different vital situations. Especially was this true in a period whose point of view in all countries was above all supranational. In the 1700's certain Spanish writers find it possible to do something new in poetry, not in spite of the rules of art and a rationalization of poetic technique but in great part due to these very rules and to the ideas like Pope's and Feijoo's on the relation of literary form to *nature* [. . . .] Above all, there has to be a re-evaluation, from within the artistic context of the Neoclassic works, of the role of eighteenth-century reform and didactic preoccupations. In some cases— especially Iriarte's apologues—*utility*, or better the *appearance of utility*, is nothing but a springboard in order to arrive at an aesthetic value.[4]

Sebold's statements propose an entirely new attitude toward the Spanish eighteenth century, an attitude in great contrast to that of Sismondi's summation. Perhaps because of the perspective of time we are at last beginning to look at Spanish literature of that time without the prejudices of old. It has finally become easier, if the critic is willing, to see attitudes and movements of the Spanish eighteenth century as neither so cold nor so exclusive in development and outlook as has been asserted for nearly two-hundred years. We can use this more open, positive attitude to good advantage as we look at the real bases of thought in Meléndez' work. We will find an intermingling of attitudes which have often been considered self-negating, i.e., Neoclassic and Romantic. If we recall the looseness of chronological development seen in eighteenth-century art and poetry in Chapter 2, we can more readily accept the same looseness of development in philosophy and poetry seen here now in Chapter 3.

Luzán's *La poética o reglas de la poesía* (*Poetics or Rules of Poetry*) has several statements in it that are quite useful at this stage in our study. By seeing something of what is in the original work, we can more adequately understand what Luzán proposed in his art of poetry and desired as a result of its appearance. His ideas are distinctly clear in the following selections:

But leaving aside what others have said, good or bad, about the essence of poetry, since we would never finish if we tried to examine here all the other definitions, we shall propose our own, for what it is worth, as best adjusted to the system of our art of poetry. We note first that *poetics is the art of composing poems and of judging them* [. . . .] It is therefore clear that it is quite a different thing from poetry. This being established, I say that poetry can be defined as *imi-*

tation of nature in a universal or particular sense done with verses for utility or for the pleasure of mankind or for both.

I say first *imitation of nature* because imitation as I have already noted is the way of poetry. Here I use the word *imitation* in its greatest extension because I want to include not only those poets who imitated in the strictest sense which is appropriate for epic and dramatic poetry—i.e., they imitated human actions—but also those who imitated in a broader sense [. . . .]

I add *in a universal or particular sense* because I believe that *imitation* can be reduced to these two designations. *Things can be portrayed or imitated either as they really are, which is to imitate the particular, or as they are according to the ideas and opinions of men, which is to imitate the universal* [italics mine . . . .]

I say *done with verses,* pointing out in this way the instrument that poetry employs, in contrast to the other arts which use colors, metal, or other instruments, but never verses. Besides this, my intention is to exclude with these words from the number of poems and from the name of poetry all prose, no matter how much it imitates human customs, emotions, or actions. And although [. . .] others, seemingly basing themselves on the authority of Aristotle, are of a contrary opinion preferring that dialogue and other types of prose that they imitate be called poetry, I nevertheless have always preferred the reasons with which verse is proved necessary to poetry. They are also confirmed by the authority of Plato, of Aristotle himself, and of many other authors of arts of poetry. If verse were not necessary, I would have no difficulty whatever in calling many passages from famous historians poetry, particularly when they refer to very old and obscure things and when they describe situations which, while quite probable, are no longer remembered [. . . .]

I say finally *for utility or for the pleasure of mankind or for both* because these are the three purposes which a poet can have, just as Horace said in his *Poetics* [. . . .] And I say this even though there are several opinions as to the ultimate goal of poetry, since some want it to be utility, others pleasure, and others think the greatest perfection of poetry consists of the mingling and union of both, again according to Horace himself [. . . .]

Nevertheless, it has seemed just and reasonable to me to admit in the number of poets those who wrote only to instruct as well as those who wrote only to entertain, as long as the pleasure is not harmful to custom or contrary to the laws of our holy faith. If one really looks well at the situation, neither is pleasure lacking in the first group because the harmony in the verse and the poetic locution supply it adequately, nor is there lacking in the other group the utility that comes from a licit and honest diversion.[5]

There are several things in this rather lengthy quotation that merit our attention. The supposed rigidity of Luzán's rules is not nearly so blatant as Sismondi, and some earlier and later critics, would have us infer. When Luzán states the necessity for poetry to be written in verse, he indirectly stresses the importance of imagination in the creative process. Imagination and fantasy may thus exist in poetry—as long as they are portrayed in verse. Luzán in one particular line opts for a kind of poetic prose—"If verse were not necessary, I would have no difficulty whatever in calling many passages from famous historians poetry, particularly when they refer to very old and obscure things and when they describe situations which, while quite probable, are no longer remembered." Where is the Neoclassic coldness and rigidity in this statement? Indeed, the sentence sounds frankly very modern in its soft emphasis on personal evocation and indirectly negates the oft-heard criticism that prosaism is supposedly inherent and therefore bad in all works of the Neoclassic school.

In the last paragraph of the quotation Luzán is quite broad in his interpretation of who really may be considered poets. Even when the poet is writing to instruct, Luzán would find "harmony in the verse" and a "poetic locution" abundant enough to provide the desired lightness and enjoyment for the reader that any good poetry should have. The Spanish critic opens up a tremendously wide source for poetry when he includes as poets those who ostensibly write only for pleasure. After all, such writers who provide nothing "harmful to custom or contrary to the laws of our holy faith" also provide the certain "utility that comes from a licit and honest diversion." It is not misunderstanding Luzán's basic intention to affirm here the freedom that exists within the very manifesto of Spanish Neoclassicism. When we can find a certain amount of freedom or looseness at the very source of a movement that has been criticized for a total lack of said quality, then we can proceed with some reason to view how other philosophies might subtly creep into the Spanish literary mentality and affect writers of the time, whether ardently Neoclassic in their outlook or not.

II *Sensationalism—Locke and Condillac*

Actually, before the appearance of Luzán's *Poetics* in 1737, the art of poetry had been undergoing vast changes, principally in the direction of more individuality on the part of the writer. This gradual change had been occurring ever since the appearance of Francis Bacon's inductive philosophy in the early seventeenth century. Somewhat later in the century the concept of personal observation inherent in this philosophy was soon joined to the concept of experience of Sir Isaac Newton's empirical physics. At the very end of the seventeenth century, John Locke expounded his sensationalist doctrine maintaining that all our knowledge originates in sensation or sense perceptions or, more precisely still, that all man's knowledge is made up of sense elements. Condillac continued Locke's philosophy in practical application to poetics within the eighteenth century itself. Sensationalism, to use one word to designate the philosophical currents just noted, was at the heart of this gradual development of poetics.

As Sebold points out in an article on the emergence of Spanish Romanticism, one of the most significant developments within the Spanish Neoclassic school was descriptive poetry.[6] The Marquis of Saint-Lambert in the *Preliminary Discourse* of his *Les Saisons* (*The Seasons*) in 1769, Sebold notes, was perhaps the first to call attention to the innovations in this poetry in the Romance countries. Saint-Lambert stresses the importance of the person, the artist, as creator. Essentially what has occurred is an acceptance of Locke's sensationalist philosophy by this time in eighteenth-century poetics. The date 1769 also marks the beginning of the period when Meléndez began to write poetry.

That nature has taken on most clearly a different meaning and relationship to man is what Saint-Lambert points out. The poet through his sensual approach to nature makes her actually a part of himself. What we find portrayed for us in a pastoral poem is not an objective description of a natural scene, but a quite subjective one based on the poet's reaction to what he sees and feels around him. It is not difficult at all to see here the basis for the literary device of nature as a universal mirror.

The philosophical basis for this relationship of man and nature can be pinpointed in John Locke's *An Essay Concerning*

Philosophy and Poetry

Human Understanding. In Book Two, Chapter Twenty-seven has the following words concerning "Personal Identity":

To find wherein personal identity consists, we must consider what *person* stands for; which, I think, is a thinking intelligent being, that has reason and reflection, and can consider itself as itself, the same thinking thing, in different times and places; which it does only by that consciousness which is inseparable from thinking, and, as it seems to me, essential to it; it being impossible for anyone to perceive without perceiving that he does perceive. When we see, hear, smell, taste, feel, meditate, or will anything, we know that we do so. Thus it is always as to our present sensations and perceptions; and by this everyone is to himself that which he calls *self* [. . . .] Since consciousness always accompanies thinking, and it is that that makes everyone to be what he calls self, and thereby distinguishes himself from all other thinking things, in this alone consists personal identity, i.e. the sameness of a rational being [. . . .] [7]

Locke continues his ideas about consciousness further on and implies the philosophical essence of the concept of nature as a universal mirror. He emphasizes the importance of the senses through the individual's ability to receive sensations—from nature or elsewhere—and store them away. The individual incorporates these sensations into his mind and creates a veritable treasure of memory which conceivably could be the source for a "romantic" revelation later on the artist's part. To see exactly what is meant here, one has only to note the power of recall in our sense of smell. How many times are we reminded of incidents even from childhood simply by the odor of a particular perfume or the smell of some flower. Immediately, the past episode returns in all its detail, but this detail does not deny a certain nostalgia the memory may provoke. Locke writes in "Consciousness Makes Personal Identity":

For as far as any intelligent being *can* repeat the idea of any past action with the same consciousness it had of it at first, and with the same consciousness it has of any present action, so far as it is the same personal self. For it is by the consciousness it has of its present thoughts and actions, that it is *self to itself* now, and so will be the same self, as far as the same consciousness can extend to actions past or to come; and would be by distance of time, or change of substance, no more two persons, than a man be two men by wearing other clothes today than he did yesterday, with a long or short sleep between; the same consciousness uniting those distant actions into the same person, whatever substances contributed to their production.[8]

One more philosopher of great importance in the eighteenth century must be noted before we go into the more literary application of the above ideas. Étienne Bonnot de Condillac wrote a work *Traité Des Sensations* (*Treatise on Sensations*) in which he describes a figure, a statue, that actually represents man in various stages of his development. Early in the work Condillac describes the statue's perception of its environment:

We imagined a statue organized internally as we are and animated with a spirit deprived of all ideas. We further supposed that the marble exterior did not permit it the use of any of its senses, and we reserved for ourselves the right to open them at our choice to the different impressions to which they are susceptible [. . . .]

The principle that determines the development of the statue's faculties is simple. The sensations themselves are the secret, for, all being necessarily pleasant or unpleasant, the statue is interested in enjoying the first and in getting rid of the second. Now, one will realize that this self-interest is sufficient to cause understanding and will to function. Judgment, reflection, desire, passion, etc. are only sensation itself which transforms itself in different directions. This is why it seemed useless to us to suppose that the soul receives immediately from nature all the faculties with which it is endowed. Nature gives us the organs to tell us through pleasure what we must look for and through pain what we must flee. But she stops there, and she leaves to experience the duty of making us form our habits and of carrying out the work which she has begun [. . . .]

[As these "habits" are gradually formed, the soul] feels as if it extends into everything. Since it sees nothing that limits it, it has only a vague feeling about its limits. Its scope or its extensiveness is totally without barriers. It seems to the statue that it itself is repeated into infinity [. . .] that it is everywhere and is everything.[9]

At the end of this quotation we find a tremendous expansion of the *self* noted in Locke's *Essay*. The statue and the world about it are molded into one entity. Such a belief is at the heart of the Romantic belief in the extreme interplay of man and nature.

In Part IV of Condillac's *Treatise*, when the statue finally possesses all its five senses, it becomes superstitious, just as man does in his environment. The statue is portrayed now as being affected by its world and thinks it must placate its environment if it is to live in peace. Still it cannot escape a certain fear of nature, of everything that surrounds it, even when it is most in love with these surroundings. At this point we might remember the threatening crags in Watteau's paintings and the ominous natural scenes in Meléndez' poetry seen in Chapter 2. Condillac portrays the statue as praying for pleasure on the one hand, and begging for deliverance from pain on the other. He writes: "It addresses the sun. Because it thinks that if the sun gives it light and warmth, it has these things as its purpose, the statue begs it to continue giving light and warmth. The statue addresses trees and asks them for their fruit [. . . .] In a word, it addresses all the things on which it believes itself dependent [. . . .] It addresses pain as if it were an invisible enemy which it must appease. Thus the universe becomes filled with visible and invisible beings which the statue begs to work for its happiness. Such are its first ideas when it begins to reflect on its state of dependence." [10]

In this quotation we find a firm basis for all the ideas concerning man and nature that developed throughout the eighteenth century. It is significant that Condillac is the first of these philosophers to live totally within the century. His words provide us an elementary framework on which to see developing Romantic attitudes. Principal among these is an essential one that insists on a closeness to nature, on a personal reaction between man and nature, and last, on a strongly personal tone that must exist in the resultant artistic creation. The evolutionary aspect of philosophical movements in the eighteenth century has become quite apparent to us. We can see now that Romantic philosophy in general had a detailed and lengthy background. The literary movement itself did not appear as if from nowhere, but began very early to partake of existing philosophies.

III *Alexander Pope*

To understand how philosophical outlooks merged so well into literary precepts, we turn to Alexander Pope. Meléndez was greatly influenced by Pope in his formative years, mainly because he could find in the Englishman's writings a basis of thought that best suited his own evolving literary criteria. Locke's sensationalist philosophy was very essential to Pope's outlook, which greatly stressed the interaction of man and nature. In his *Essay on Man,* Pope presents the concept of a man who enters a preordained, limited nature. His view does not suppose the omnipotence of man over himself and his world. Pope sees a universe beautiful in its entirety, controlled by a wise, loving God. There will be dissension in it, for after all man is a passionate animal, but such a situation is not necessarily unfortunate or even unharmonious:

> Better for us, perhaps, it might appear,
> Were there all harmony, all virtue here;
> That never air or ocean felt the wind,
> That never passion discomposed the mind:
> But all subsists by elemental strife;
> And passions are the elements of life.
> The gen'ral order, since the whole began,
> Is kept in Nature, and is kept in Man.[11]

In this universe the interaction of man and nature is doubly stressed in the following verses. Man's part in this whole is rather bluntly and cynically established:

> Just as absurd to mourn the tasks or pains
> The great directing Mind of All ordains.
> All are but parts of one stupendous Whole,
> Whose body Nature is, and God the soul [. . . .]
> All Nature is but Art unknown to thee;
> All chance direction, which thou canst not see;
> All discord, harmony not understood;
> All partial evil, universal good;
> And spite of Pride, in erring Reason's spite,
> One truth is clear, *Whatever is, is right* [. . . .]
> Know then thyself, presume not God to scan,
> The proper study of mankind is Man [. . . .]
> Born but to die, and reas'ning but to err;
> Alike in ignorance, his reason such,
> Whether he thinks too little or too much;
> Chaos of thought and passion, all confused;
> Still by himself abused or disabused;
> Created half to rise, and half to fall;
> Great Lord of all things, yet a prey to all;
> Sole judge of truth, in endless error hurl'd;
> The glory, jest, and riddle of the world!
> Go, wondrous creature! mount where Science guides;

Go, measure earth, weigh air, and state the tides [. . . .]
Go, teach Eternal Wisdom how to rule—
Then drop into thyself, and be a fool! [12]

A more direct literary influence came to Meléndez from another of Pope's works, his *An Essay on Criticism*, written in 1709 when Pope was just twenty years old. Pope portrays nature as the beginning and end, the fountainhead of art. But, remembering his concept of the universe controlled by a benign Supreme Being, Pope portrays nature as ordered. The idea of nature "methodized," probably Pope's most memorable proclamation concerning aesthetics, is what we find in this work. Art and nature, from this point of view, come closer and closer together. In the restrained freedom of nature, as it were, we nevertheless find the beginnings of that wild, primitive, and rampant nature of the Romantics of the early nineteenth century. The following lines indicate what we mean here:

First follow Nature, and your judgment frame
By her just standard, which is still the same;
Unerring Nature, still divinely bright,
One clear, unchanged, and universal light,
Life, force, and beauty must to all impart,
At once the source, and end, and test of Art [. . . .]
Those rules of old, discover'd not devised,
Are Nature still, but Nature methodized;
Nature, like Liberty, is but restrain'd
By the same laws which first herself ordain'd [italics mine. . . .]
Some beauties yet no precepts can declare,
For there's a happiness as well as care.
Music resembles poetry; in each
Are nameless graces which no methods teach [. . . .]
If, where the rules not far enough extend,
(Since rules were made but to promote their end)
Some lucky license answer to the full
Th'intent proposed, that license is a rule.
Thus Pegasus, a nearer way to take,
May boldly deviate from the common track [italics mine].[13]

In this long quotation, the relationship of man, nature, and art is precisely delineated. Of most importance is the assertion that nature and art are essentially on the same plane. The philos-

[99]

opher or the poet, attempting to reach the essence of beauty, concentrates totally on the object of inspiration. He is guided by his senses in this concentration and in this way he approaches the object from a personal standpoint, herein emphasizing once more the sensationalist philosophy of Locke, later so aptly developed by Condillac. So far the philosopher-poet is not permitted to wander aimlessly in his admiration, however. His mind is controlled by certain internal regulations or restraints much as nature is controlled within the universe from on high. The work of art is not perceived as something cold, outside the artist's mind and spirit, but something vibrant and alive whose production is the fruition of beauty. To reach this fruition, the philosopher-poet is allowed to follow his instincts when existing rules do not adequaltely permit satisfying self-expression. Such intent is obvious in Pope's last lines above. We found an indication of this freedom in the lines quoted from Luzán earlier in this chapter. From a very early date, with both Pope and Luzán, in Western European Neoclassicism, we are thus moving toward the more personal, subjective philosophy of full-blown Romanticism of the nineteenth century. Writers thus realize quite early that artistic norms originate in man's own taste and do not necessarily have to come from Antique rules and models for imitation. We must comprehend this fluidity of philosophy at work if we are to understand how Meléndez, for example, and other Spaniards or non-Spaniards, could be at the same time "Neoclassic" and "Romantic." The two systems of thought do not negate each other at all, but rather flow back and forth from one to the other.

IV Incipient Influence on Meléndez

From early in his philosophical development Meléndez had known the works discussed above. Georges Demerson points out that these works were in Meléndez' library.[14] Meléndez himself, in a letter written to Jovellanos from Salamanca in 1776, tells us just how important Locke was in the formation of his own philosophical directions:

I am learning the English language with an indescribable zeal and tenacity. The grammar book I use is the English-French one by M. Peyton. More than anything my frequent encounters with two young Irishmen of this school are helping me. They were raised in London

Philosophy and Poetry

and thus have no Irish accent. I am translating some things already
and I understand quite well the colloquial pronunciation of the letters.
I earnestly hope that some day I can carry on my correspondence with
you in English to show my esteem for your advice through my rapid
advance in that language. Ever since I was a child I have had an excessive admiration for the English language and literature. One of the
first books I received, and which I learned by heart, was by a very
learned Englishman. To the *Essay Concerning Human Understanding*
I owe, and shall always owe, my ability to think and reason.[15]

Remembering Locke's ideas and those of the other philosophers
mentioned and what Meléndez fervently tells us above, we shall
examine how Meléndez incorporates them into his own and brings
about a new literary outlook in Spain. Several critics have hinted
at Meléndez' importance in the development of Spanish Romanticism. Sebold, in his article on the emergence of that movement,
refers most positively to Meléndez' role in this regard. So far
he has usually been considered an important Spanish pre-Roman-
tic, but it is necessary actually to recognize him as the founder of
Romanticism in Spanish literature. By asserting his tremendous
significance in this role, we shall again be emphasizing the
inherently evolutionary character of the movement. Such recognition naturally opposes the more traditional criticism wherein
Meléndez is portrayed as a frivolous antecedent of the Romantics
of the 1830's and 1840's. By accepting Meléndez' real importance
in the evolution of Spanish poetry, we shall espouse too a freer,
more healthy attitude toward the eighteenth century and what its
real significance is in Spanish literature.

Azorín is the first critic to wonder cogently about Meléndez'
importance as a Romantic poet. He writes in a series of essays
De Granada a Castelar (*From Granada to Castelar*) in 1922:

From time to time one thinks about the origins of Spanish Romanticism. They have been recently discussed because of the intention to
found a Museum of Romanticism. What are the origins of Romanticism in Spain? From what basis can we find such an aesthetic movement springing? And what precursors shall we assign to the systemat-
ically declared Romantics? The Romantic movement in Spain and in
France has roots deep in the eighteenth century. In France those an-
tecedents have been carefully studied, but in Spain [. . . .] they have
not been studied yet [. . . .] There is one author who has carried out in
Spain Chateaubriand's mission in France [. . . .] We are alluding to

Meléndez Valdés. How is it that when speaking of the Romantic movement in Spain Meléndez Valdés is never cited? All of Romanticism is
already contained—impetuous and fiery—in Meléndez. In him we find
the pronounced subjectivism of the Romantics: the melancholy, the
solemn emphasis, the unevenness between idea and expression, the
taste for horrible spectacles, the tenderness, the tears, and the infinite
despair.[16]

In a sort of background summary quoted below, Azorín provides the essential reasons for Meléndez' outlook. His words echo
the sentiments seen particularly in Locke and Pope. The idea
Azorín advances in great part is also that of the more serious
interpretation of the Rococo spirit we stressed in Chapter 2. In
brief, Azorín views Meléndez as a sufferer of the disillusion inherent in any sensitive person of the Baroque and Rococo periods:

A great sentimental revolution was being announced. The eighteenth
century criticized everything: emotions, ideas, institutions. Everything
was belittled, pulverized, and destroyed. [Azorín is perhaps a little
too zealous here. He expresses an attitude about the period that has
become very popular in our century, however.] Actually the only thing
that remained sublime was the personality of the critic; that is, the "I"
that considers and examines everything [. . . .] Meléndez arrives at
this moment of universal disintegration [. . . .] The poet finds himself
all alone, despairing, agonizing at the ruin of all old beliefs and feelings. What can he lean on? What does the future hold in store for
him? To whom can he turn? [17]

Azorín goes on to say that everything found in the Romanticism of the nineteenth century is found in Meléndez. The only
thing not really visible is a sense of the picturesque, the return
to the Middle Ages for inspiration, and the taste for the archaic.
"And that is the only way in which later Romantics—Zorrilla,
Rivas, García Gutiérrez—have surpassed him. Meléndez brought
everything else to art: lyrical exaltation, shattering melancholy,
and the richness and profusion of a dictionary." [18]

To emphasize the richness of Meléndez' work and the resultant wide range of interpretation it provides, I have chosen
to start our examination of his literary philosophy with an
Anacreontic ode studied in Chapter 2. It then provided an example of the wealth of emotions and attitudes in this one particular type of poetry. The poem can be used this time to show the

lightness that Meléndez' openly philosophical poems can contain. The ode, Number XXVII, "On Science," tells of the feeling of desolation caused by Meléndez' study of the sciences. We considered it earlier as testimony of his inherent desire to escape, the basic wish of the Rococo artist. The flippancy of the last strophe again concerns us. Meléndez attempts to laugh away his preoccupations of the first strophes. He wants us to believe the apparent banality at the end and accept it as his true feelings. The mixture of playfulness and seriousness is so common in his poems that at times the reader is not certain of the poet's emphasis. This seeming confusion has also been one more reason for critics to dismiss his work at times as being artificial. In this particular poem, the final playfulness heightens the poet's feeling of disillusion and despair in the first strophes. He is indeed calling for wine and song, but in a vain attempt to avoid stresses that were only too real for him. The idea of escape is definitely here, with very serious emotional implications:

> I applied myself to the sciences,
> Thinking in their truths
> To find an easy remedy
> For all my ills.
> Oh, what a silly illusion! [. . . .]
> Then, bring me wine, my shepherd girl;
> For as long as I have it,
> Do not fear that
> My happy songs will cease.[19]

The playful, boyish refusal to learn, to be serious is, of course, only one side of Meléndez' personality. In many poems it is not visible at all. A good example within the *Anacreontic Odes* is Number III, "A una fuente" ("To a Fountain"), which in a very lyrical, musical style shows in the first strophe the close relationship between man and nature. The senses and their importance to the poet are emphasized in the word *espíritu* (*spirit, soul*) in the third line of the quotation below. The poet is not objective in his presentation of nature, but internalizes his reactions created from the former sensations. The naturalness of Meléndez' expression and the poetic image itself are a succinct indication of Locke's sensationalist philosophy and its role in the poet's writing. The image of the pool mirroring the poet's *soul—*

not his face, his external self—implies how profoundly his senses have perceived nature. His soul and nature actually interact on a common level. A certain continuity in the development of Spanish poetry can also be seen in the evocative simplicity of the wording and the subject itself which remind us of some early poems of Machado. Meléndez writes: "Oh! how much in your crystal depths,/ Smiling little fountain,/ Does my *spirit* [italics mine] delight in itself,/ Do my eyes become enraptured!" [20]

The clearest, purest expression, perhaps, of his serious side is found in the last poem included in the *BAE* collection. It is his Discourse III, "Orden del universo, y cadena admirable de sus seres: Dedicado a Jovellanos" ("Order of the Universe and Admirable Chain of Its Beings: Dedicated to Jovellanos"). It is a long, sober panegyric to the order conceived by the Supreme Being for His universe. The sciences, all human study, are rightly praised as contributing to maintain the symmetry of this divine order. I believe that the poem brings out more concisely than any other one poem by Meléndez all the inherited sensationalist characteristics we have been discussing.

The first verses immediately recall the first quotations from Pope's *Essay on Man*. The general order of the universe through nature is quite positively stressed. The poet's sensualist means of comprehending this order—the poet raises his eyes to the heavens—is definitely Lockean in origin. Meléndez writes:

> My soul expires admiring
> The heights of your ordered structure,
> Oh incomprehensible, oh great nature!
> I raise my eyes to the sky, and sparkling
> Suns without number on thrones of gold I see
> Whirling over my reeling head.
> A mad, curious desire wants to reach them,
> To direct its steps toward them, to find
> Their final cause and sovereign employ.[21]

The humility expressed in subsequent verses of the poem is reminiscent of Pope's insistent call for man to remember his place and not presume to usurp the Creator's:

> Everything is in harmony:
> The world a chain offers

> Of immense links to the quiet
> Meditator; study it and humble
> Your face before the Lord who has made it.[22]

While reflecting the attitudes of both Locke and Pope, Meléndez also presents some announcements of his own more Romantic outlook wherein his longing for solitude, for a hermetic escape, even from his questioning here, manifests itself. His words are lyrically personal, universal, and isolationist all at the same time:

> How happy in the middle of the dark night,
> On the soft grass reclining,
> Did I love to count the endless lights! [. . . .]
> The tender flowers that my body crushed,
> Immersed me in delicious amber;
> At a distance the nightingale trilled sadly;
> The august solitude, the mysterious
> Silence, the darkness, the noise
> Of the soft dawn through the leafy forest
> Absorbed me in ecstasy,
> And a supreme power filled
> My soul, now liberated from the vileness of earth.[23]

The poet goes on to marvel at all facets of the universe and at how well they interact together. In the concluding strophes, he is so carried away by the perfection of the universe, of his world that he senses about him, that he goes into an ecstasy of emotion and imagines such harmony existing on and on into infinity. In the very last strophe, he even says that if reason alone is not enough, then man's hope will assure him the continuance of the perfection about him. This poem very nicely elaborates the earlier eighteenth-century philosophies we have noted and expresses also a totally personal, exuberant one. Meléndez' ability to portray himself emotionally in his work is especially evident here where there is an emphasis on the capacity for man's intelligence, the sciences or reason, nature, and man's hope all to work together. In one line ("[. . .]my soul/ Becomes lost contemplating a single flower") there is even an important anticipation of William Blake's "To see a World in a Grain of Sand/ And a Heaven in a Wild Flower." Blake's editor dates these lines about 1803;

Meléndez' poem was written before June, 1795. The last strophes
read in part:

Who fabricated the proportions of such a
Structure, so distant? Who, the harmony
Of such a whole, its ends, its beauty?
I become confused, I become lost: my soul
Becomes lost contemplating a single flower,
One of many happy May creates.
What will become of it
If taking flight up to the skies,
My soul sees many more suns and worlds spread out there
All revolving around a common center;
And this one and those all directed
By a single law, and perhaps on them
Millions of beings. . . . Oh, where am I going lost?
But, then, is not the great Being powerful enough to make them?
Is he perhaps incapable of the greatest knowledge?
For what reason these beautiful stars?
Is such a gift only for the earth? . . . .
Since reason, Jovino, cannot reach its highest destiny,
Let hope at least seek on.[24]

A poem very similar in tone is found in the *Philosophical and
Sacred Odes.* Ode III, "A un lucero" ("To a Bright Star"), has
the same intellectual and emotional wonderment in it as the
discourse above, but at the end it is even more personal in its
nostalgic evocation of loneliness, of the poet's oneness in the
world. He can see a physical thing, the star, and can meditate
upon its ethereal implications, but it in itself is not enough to
console him if he is distressed. In fact, it, through its very
capriciousness, can precipitate a melancholy in him that at the
beginning of the poem was unimaginable. Visibly, then, Meléndez' own personality influences his view of the world, of nature,
and causes him to fear what originally was pleasant. At this point
we see the concept of nature as a universal mirror, the pathetic
fallacy, at a somewhat elementary but critical stage of development. Meléndez writes:

With what pleasure do I look at you,
From my peaceful room,
Oh beautiful star,

Who shine over my head! [. . . .]
How in the gloomy night
With sweet violence do you fix
My ecstatic eyes on yourself,
And with your brilliance do you betwitch me! [. . . .]
However it was the divine Newton,
Who raising himself
To the heights of the empyrean,
Where the great Being lives,
From Him learned happily
The admirable law that joins
The forces of the universe
With an eternal knot
And makes them in the immense ether [. . .]
Follow the same course.
The angels were astonished
That human daring
Could reach where they hardly
With arduous labor can go [. . . .]
Why do you [stars] turn
In different directions? Why, united
Like a great army, do you not form
A single line?
Why? . . . . My mind is overwhelmed,
And as it looks above admiringly,
It finds more and more
To admire as it meditates.
But my beautiful star,
Where is it? What became of
Its brightly-lit flame?
Who, oh, deprives me of my love?
While I rendered the homage due
Such a sun [. . .]
It sank into the black shadows [. . . .] [25]

Ode IV, "La presencia de Dios" ("The Presence of God"), comes immediately after the above poem in the *BAE* collection. It is a further elaboration of Discourse II and Ode III that we have just quoted. It is closer to the discourse in its marveling at the symmetry of the universe wisely directed by a benign supreme power. In Ode IV there is no doubt or creeping despair that is intimated in the last verses of Ode III. Ode IV begins: "Wherever I turn/ My eyes, anxious in my desire,/ There, my Lord!, present/ Does my astonished soul feel you." [26]

In the next poem, the last to be included in this section of our chapter, we note the total disruption of the order seen in the previously quoted poems. The poem is another of the *Philosophical and Sacred Odes* (Number XXIII) and is appropriately entitled "El fanatismo" ("Fanaticism"). Godoy, in his *Memorias* (*Memoirs*), refers to it at one point, commenting on its appropriateness and the poet's fine sensibility. He uses the poem to show the difficulties that his government experienced in its fight against reactionary elements.[27] Meléndez, writing in early 1794 against the evils he sees around him daily, is no longer able to see a world justly ordered by a benign ruler. Man's own weakness has precipitated the chaos the poet portrays. The poet can no longer achieve that former ethereal tranquillity of the preceding poems. He is on the verge of slipping into the deep depression to be seen in the poetry of the next section. In the midst of this new stage of philosophical development it is amusing to see the dilettantish attitude in the reference to the recently unearthed city of Pompeii. The verses below express a quite personal, emotional viewpoint that in a minor key announces the more morbid paintings of Goya, especially his *Colossus* or *Panic*:

> The heavens, outraged, thundered,
> And their highest poles shook
> Over the blind mortals [. . .]
> Who abandoned the God of the Universe [. . . .]
> [The heavens] threw to earth in her misfortune
> Bloody fanaticism [. . . .]
> Thus the monster once [. . .]
> Its great chest writhing
> Inflamed Vesuvius [. . .]
> And covered with a wide sea of burning lava
> The rich earth of Pompeii [. . . .]
> What is this, eternal Author
> Of this sad world? Does your sublime name
> Which is now insulted no longer moderate passions? [. . . .]
> Suddenly in a dark cloud
> The desolated land was submerged
> And genius and virtue were obliterated;
> Their divine beauty
> The quarrelsome sciences

Bewailed among shadows [. . .]
And, his conscience filled
With a thousand fearsome superstitions,
Man found his unhappy shackles doubled.[28]

V *Pathetic Fallacy*

The specific relationship of man and nature in Meléndez'
poetry is what will concern us in the next several pages. We have
discussed the philosophical foundation for the relationship and
have noted its appearance. What we find basically in this relationship is nature innocent and pure, acting as a sort of refuge
for man in his escape from the too real world of his everyday
life. The idea sounds not unlike that of the *beatus ille*, yet in
Meléndez' new outlook man becomes at times an almost pitiable
creature who looks for succor from a kind of maternal being.
There were other writers who expressed this literary viewpoint
and who conceivably influenced Meléndez. Principal among them
were James Thomson with his *Seasons* (1726–1730) and the
Marquis of Saint-Lambert with his *The Seasons* mentioned earlier.

Even though this closeness of man and nature with the resultant
concept of nature's innocence is usually considered Rousseauistic
in tone, the philosophy had really been developing since John
Locke's day. Locke's sensationalist philosophy proposed essentially an independent position for man wherein nature did not
directly determine his feelings, but became, instead, an extension
of his consciousness. The basic idea is that man turns to nature
for consolation just as Condillac's statue did. This attitude, developed in the eighteenth century and not the nineteenth, we
see, forms the nucleus of the concept of pathetic fallacy or
of nature as a universal mirror. We can now look at certain of
Meléndez' poems to see how he expresses it, its expression being
one step further toward his emergence as the earliest of the truly
Romantic Spanish poets.

Ode XVIII of the *Philosophical and Sacred Odes* is entitled
"A las estrellas" ("To the Stars"). It is an invocation of sorts to
the universe, but this time the poet is not happy contemplating
God's world as he was in some poems we previously quoted. In
the very first strophe he appears totally lost on facing the natural
manifestations of the world about him:

Where am I? what rapid flight
Of winged intelligence raises me
From this vile earth to the royal
Palaces of the heavens?
Stop, brilliant suns,
Eternal lamps,
Who flee revolving in such lightness [. . . .] [29]

Meléndez becomes so confused by the immensity of all he sees,
that he imagines more and greater stellar systems. This thought,
somewhat more veiled in previous quotations, here becomes too
much for him and, rather than elating him, throws him into a
profound despair:

Where, glorious suns,
Is this *beyond* that I never see?
Will one daring soul never conquer
The mysterious limits
Of this ineffable empire,
No matter how earnest,
It may advance in its desire?
Ah! Nature, limitless, will always
Overwhelm man cowering in his miserable lowness.
Always, sacred lights,
You will burn; the human mind
Will follow your golden flight
With feeble wings,
And will fall, breathless.
Mysterious night
Will hang with her shining veil
Over the wide firmament,
And I, intoxicated in my pleasant error,
Shall turn, anxious, to my happy cares.[30]

The insignificance of self—greatly enhanced in the ironic language of the last verses—that the poet feels, the tremendous
power of nature, and the fearsome yet pleasant intoxication he
receives from his contemplation are all a part of the new relationship between man and nature.

The above attitude is further reflected in Ode XIII, "La
tempestad" ("The Storm") in a more subtle way. Seemingly
directed at God in his omnipotence, the poem is really a praise of
nature and its awesome, terrifying powers:

> It thunders again; the Lord
> Is approaching; his throne
> In the middle of the storm he places.
> Desolation follows him,
> And the lightning only awaits his voice [. . . .] [31]

The powerful destruction of which nature is capable comes out forcefully in Ode XVI, "La noche de invierno" ("Winter Night"). The poet's attraction to this power is quite striking. The influence of Thomson, seen in the subject and wording at times, is also seen in the hypnotic rapture that overtakes the poet as he is released this time from the tranquility of self into the fury of nature around him. The important thing is that he is carried away from himself into an isolation that only he can experience. Nature has reached into his most inner being and brought out from his subconscious all the frustrations and anger he feels within. Nature's ability to provide purgation, refuge, and consolation is, of course, at the basis of the concept of nature as a universal mirror. Note the pent-up anger in the poet and the paradoxically calming effect the storm has on him in the following lines:

> Oh how horribly do the winds hit
> Each other! Oh what whistling,
> Which disturbs sky and earth
> With infuriated blasts! [. . . .]
> Oh winter! Oh sad night!
> How welcome in my tranquil
> Breast is your horror! your thunder
> How placid to my ear [. . . .]
> Oh immense Being! oh first
> Cause! Where, arrogantly,
> With reckless flight,
> Does my delirium carry me? [. . . .] [32]

The importance of solitude and night, as parts of nature, stands out very well in Ode IX, "La noche y la soledad" ("Night and Solitude"), written in 1779. Nature is at a further stage of development in the poet's mind in this instance and reflects not so much Thomson or Saint-Lambert as Edward Young in his *Night Thoughts.* There may very well be, too, an influence from

Cadalso's *Noches lúgubres* (*Lugubrious Nights*). In his poem
Meléndez seeks out the solitude nature provides. The somewhat
sepulchral tone is significant here and recalls Young, whom
Meléndez cites by name. The consoling effect of solitude is
emphasized when it calms a troubled heart. The poem begins:

> Come, sweet solitude, and my soul
> Free from the horrisonant, agitated sea
> Of the corrupt world,
> And return peace and happiness
> To my suffering, wounded heart;
> Come, raise my beaten spirit [. . . .]
> You, august solitude, fill my soul
> With another sublime light; you separate it
> From pestilent pleasure,
> And while in silence you transport it,
> You prepare it for virtue [. . . .] [33]

At one point in the poem the *beatus-ille* theme joins with
another theme so typical of the eighteenth century—that of
virtue. It is not surprising to come upon the theme of friendship
further on in the poem since it was considered the principal means
of achieving virtue among the Salamancan poets. The poem is
dedicated to Jovellanos, and it is to him Meléndez speaks in words
greatly reminiscent of Fray Luis de León in the following
verses:

> When will come the day, bright and pure,
> That in gentle solitude joined with you
> My anxious soul
> Can dry its tears,
> Where free in the most solitary and hidden forest
> And at the foot of the most leafy tree,
> In celestial repose
> May we contemplate such sublime truths?
> Hasten, oh heavens!, such days,
> And let us play the funereal cither,
> Oh, Young, that you played [. . . .] [34]

The idea of the above lines is emphasized in the last verses
of the poem where a sort of ethereal peace is achieved. Solitude
draws the poet and Jovellanos to nature's bosom. The inherent

sadness and melancholy are once more stressed by the reference to Young. Nature does more here than merely reflect the poet's inner longings for peace. Through his projection of himself and his friend on to nature, he makes nature his own, his very self. This kind of interaction between man and nature is what Locke had in mind. Meléndez addresses Jovellanos in these words:

> You, gentle friend, who know the value
> Of meditation, and how much the soul
> Gains through solitude,
> Come [. . .]
> And with Young let us silently enter
> In soft peace these lonely places,
> Where in their sublime nights let us meditate
> A thousand divine truths,
> And moved by their lamenting voices,
> Let us repeat their lugubrious moans.[35]

The last poem included in this section is Ode XXVII, "En la desgraciada muerte del Coronel Don José Cadalso" ("On the Unfortunate Death of Colonel José Cadalso"), written but never completed shortly after Cadalso's death in 1782. I include it because the references to solitude and death which might elsewhere be more influenced by a conscious imitation of Young are here elicited from a true feeling of despair and isolation at the loss of his friend and mentor. The relationship of nature and poet is quite close here, to the point this time that the poet realizes his insignificance in a metaphor that recalls the old "life-is-a-river" theme so well expressed in Spanish literature by Jorge Manrique in the fifteenth century. The stoicism of that earlier poem is lost, however, in the despairing attempts to recall Cadalso from the dead in the last verse quoted below. Interestingly, these same verses remind one very much of Tediato's cries in Cadalso's *Lugubrious Nights*. The lines provide a good summary of Meléndez' concept of nature—a very personal, loving-fearing, ethereal one:

> August silence, frightful forests,
> Deep valleys, shadowy solitude,
> High bare rocks,
> Who show only horrifying precipices

To my excited fantasy! [. . . .]
Your saddest and most funereal dwelling,
Where is it? and the darkest labyrinth,
Where my melancholy,
Accompanied by silence and pain,
May lose itself freely? My sorrow
Flees from the annoying light of day
And song and happiness,
As a bird of the night flees the golden sun [. . . .]
Terrible eternity! vast ocean,
Where everything becomes lost! What is life,
Compared to you? [. . . .]
Dear image! beloved friend!
Dalmiro, my Dalmiro! cold shadow!
Wait, stop,
I shall embrace your body; I shall give it warmth;
I shall lend you my breath; my soul,
Split in two, shall give you life. . . .
Insane imagination!
Vain illusion! . . . .[36]

In summary, so far in this chapter we have seen how the different philosophical attitudes of the eighteenth century, particularly that of sensationalism, began to change Meléndez' early Neoclassic outlook. At first Meléndez exhibits a contemplation of the universe wherein he views nature along the openly sensualist lines of John Locke. He then progresses in the last poem quoted to more an immersion into this universe through nature. At this point he tends to lose himself totally in nature, which either allows him to elaborate his emotions, making them universal, or merely to draw them forth in a sort of catharsis, thus giving vent to his deepest fears. This experience is the heart of the concept of pathetic fallacy.

VI "Fastidio Universal"

Meléndez from here goes further in his developing relation of poet and nature and introduces the most important of all Romantic theories—that of *mal du siècle* or as we should call it now, at least regarding Spanish literature, *fastidio universal*. To see how Meléndez develops this theory and with it further brings about the birth of Spanish Romanticism, we shall look at several more poems in this last section of the present chapter.

Philosophy and Poetry

We must first emphasize the inherent tenderness Meléndez exhibits in his poetry. Many critics have used his sensitivity as a basis for saying he was a weak man. I believe we can convincingly say now that such statements are not at all founded in real fact. This tenderness of Meléndez is principally what allowed him to escape the Neoclassic aesthetic and receive new philosophical waves that had developed in his century. The first poem we shall examine is Ode XXXIII, "Que no son flaqueza la ternura y el llanto" ("Tenderness and Tears Are Not Weakness"). It is a declaration of the necessity for the poet's own particular creative attitude and a strong defense of his sensitive, lachrymose side. The love Meléndez had for his fellowman, his humanitarianism, is also notable in the verses below:

> Do you marvel that I cry;
> That my gentle breast
> Breaks forth in a rain of tears,
> And so fervently implores Heaven?
> Not an effeminate weakness
> Nor a dull cowardliness
> Are the cause of my crying; for my soul
> Knows how to suffer with strict constancy [. . . .]
> Everywhere I look
> In eternal suffering
> I find man moaning; from my compassion
> My tears are born, and because of his pain I sigh [. . . .]
> It has not been conceded
> To me to hold back, friend, my tears [. . . .]
> And he who grieves forgotten,
> Whether in ominous exile,
> Or trembles at the barbarous power of calumny or envy
> That oppresses him,
> My breast open
> He will always find for his troubles,
> Always my tongue full of solace,
> And my face covered with tears.
> Others may applaud
> Their insensitive firmness,
> And like rocks inaccessible to compassion,
> May laugh at the sad person who weeps with other sad people;
> I, however, destined by heaven
> With the gift of my tenderness,

If I do not succeed in alleviating misfortune,
At least achieve the celestial consolation of tears.[37]

Very much in tone with this poem is Elegy V "Mis combates" ("My Combats"). The internal conflicts that are sometimes flippantly dismissed in other poems are here analyzed. Several literary motifs appear, one of the most beautifully expressed being the *ubi sunt* toward the end (which we do not quote). The sensitive, almost heartrending torments the poet feels create a deep sympathy in the reader:

> What sedition, oh Heavens, do I feel in me,
> For divided into opposing bands,
> My mind fights against itself! [. . . .]
> Is man at times told that he was made
> For this humble, fragile earth
> Where a beast is hardly satisfied?
> Man! Immortal being! so despicable
> Do you want to become? Raise your heart,
> And be for once praiseworthy in your ambition.
> What most blindly you desire, what enchants
> Your fascinated eyes, how unworthy
> It is in your light, oh, holy virtue! [. . . .]
> A soul that busies itself, that employs itself
> In the nothingness of the world, is a star
> Fallen from heaven to the mud that defaces it.
> Virtue, virtue: let this be the first
> Of your efforts, of your mind
> The study, of your heart the sincere desire,
> Of your happiness the perennial fountain.[38]

Meléndez' emotionalism, his fine sensitivity, and his love for friends and mankind in general all can become, conversely, a great burden on him in certain circumstances. Idyll VII "A la amistad" ("To Friendship") shows how the external world can overpower the poet and leave him desolate. Nature is virtually incapable of helping even when taking him to her bosom:

> In the middle of the shadows,
> Which with cold silence
> Listen compassionately
> To his laments,

> Was unhappy
> Batilo bewailing
> The painful absence
> Of all his friends.[39]

The subtle juxtaposition of the words "cold silence" and "compassionately" show us nature's ambience very nicely. The rest of the poem points out how there is only one thing—friendship —left for him before he lapses into complete despair. Later this salvation too will disappear precipitating him into a pit of self-doubt, frustration, and hopelessness. The following verses delineate the poet's mood clearly before his fall:

> I find consolation in nothing;
> For everything I see,
> Quite far from helping me,
> Only doubles my pain.
> Happiness fled like a shadow,
> And at the edge of an abyss
> Bottomless with troubles,
> I find myself suddenly.
> Sublime God! who can
> Help me in such a conflict?
> Who will be moved
> By my sad cries?
> Holy friendship! you alone,
> With a divine balsam,
> Heal the wounds
> Of a faltering spirit,
> And with a benign hand
> Touching my breast,
> Calm it, calm
> Its harsh storms.[40]

The sentiments expressed above lead naturally into those of one of Meléndez' most popular poems, Ode XXIV, "A la Mañana, en mi desamparo y orfandad" ("To Morning, on My Abandonment and Orphanhood"). The structure itself of the piece is, first of all, interesting. The poem is divided into approximately two equal parts. The first contains one of the most beautiful descriptions of morning that Meléndez ever wrote. The second part is a description of the poet in his despair. The beauty of morning is

JUAN MELÉNDEZ VALDÉS

bluntly contrasted with his own feelings of desolation. A poem by
the Duke of Rivas, "El faro de Malta" ("The Lighthouse of
Malta"), is greatly reminiscent in its structure of that of Meléndez' poem. The basic sentiments are not too different either,
although the nineteenth-century poet feels abandoned because of
political exile from Spain. Meléndez' reason is more a familial,
personal one—the death of his brother. The description of nature
is exquisite in several places and recalls some of the beautiful
descriptions noted in Chapter 2 of this book:

> In nacre clouds morning,
> Watering the withered earth with pearls,
> Approaches from the east;
> Her cheeks roselike,
> Of a candescent light her transparent veil,
> And much purer than jasmine her face.
> With her whiteness she does not permit
> The sad mantle of opaque night
> Or its squadron of bright stars
> To wrap the earth in blindness and fear;
> But with light steps,
> Spreading her divine and pure light,
> She goes forcing them into the dark west.

> (Entre nubes de nácar la mañana,
> De aljófares regando el mustio suelo,
> Asoma por oriente;
> Las mejillas de grana,
> De luz candente el trasparente velo,
> Y muy más pura que el jazmín la frente.
> Con su albor no consiente
> Que de la opaca noche al triste manto,
> Ni su escuadra de fúlgidos luceros
> La tierra envuelva en ceguedad y espanto;
> Mas con pasos ligeros,
> La luz divina y pura dilatando,
> Los va al ocaso umbrífero lanzando.) [41]

The message of the more personal second part is what most
intrigues us in the poem. Meléndez feels completely alone and
has fallen into that pit of total despair toward which he has all
along been heading. At his entrance into the abyss he appears

somewhat stoic. He is desolated, but stands firm in the following verses:

> I alone, miserable, whom the skies
> Afflict so seriously, with the dawn
> Do not feel happiness,
> But rather more grief [. . . .]
> Nor can I, oh!, stop my moaning,
> An orphan, young, alone and helpless.
>
> *(Yo sólo, ¡miserable! a quien el cielo*
> *Tan gravemente aflige, con la aurora*
> *No siento ¡ay! alegría,*
> *Sino más desconsuelo [. . . .]*
> *Ni yo ¡ay! puedo cesar en mi gemido,*
> *Huérfano, joven, solo y desvalido.)*[42]

Meléndez' pose before the universe awaiting some sort of consolation in the last line above recalls Condillac's statue standing before nature for the same reason. This attitude is particularly evident in the last poem we shall note and clearly reflects the reshaping of nature in the image of the poet's own psyche. This final poem is Elegy II, "El melancólico, a Jovino" ("The Melancholy One, to Jovino") in which the term *fastidio universal* first occurs. The date is 1794, long before the terms *mal du siècle* or *Weltschmerz*, the more common names for this phenomenon, ever appeared.[43] The importance of the senses in this change of outlook is absolute. At this stage of expectant confrontation, nature shares the poet's feelings and eventually merges with him to become one. And here we are at the universalization of the Romantic poet's grief. The poet is actually supreme at last. He is the creator of everything—his view of nature, his mood, and his verses. In so many words, he is definitively the author of his pathetic fallacy. He achieves this ultimate situation through a particular state of mind—through what Meléndez calls *fastidio universal*. In this state, the individual sufferer experiences frustration, despair, and a loss of personal initiative for the positive. This last poem now explicitly shows us how Meléndez himself feels at this emotional level. The first verses immediately set his tone:

> When the funereal shadow and the mourning
> Of the gloomy night envelop the world

In silence and horror; when in tranquil
Repose mortals the delights
Of a calm, healthful dream enjoy;
Your friend alone, bathed in tears,
Keeps watch, Jovino, and to the doubtful brightness
Of a feeble light, in sad laments,
With you alleviates his profound pain [. . . .]
You judge me happy. . . . Oh! if you could
See the deep wound in my breast,
Which pours forth blood night and day!

(*Cuando la sombra fúnebre y el luto*
De la lóbrega noche el mundo envuelven
En silencio y horror; cuando en tranquilo
Reposo los mortales las delicias
Gustan de un blando saludable sueño;
Tu amigo solo, en lágrimas bañado,
Vela, Jovino, y al dudoso brillo
De una cansada luz, en tristes ayes,
Contigo alivia su dolor profundo [. . . .]
Tú me juzgas feliz. . . . ¡Oh si pudieras
Ver de mi pecho la profunda llaga,
Que va sangre vertiendo noche y día! [44]

After this revelation of what his inner self is like, far different
from what his external appearance indicates, Meléndez gives
more description. At the end of the poem he compares himself
to "An unfortunate who into the abyss, which he flees,/ Sees
himself pulled by an invincible impulse,/ And burning with
criminal anguish,/ His heart longs for virtue" ("A un desdichado
que al abismo, que huye,/ Se ve arrastrar por invencible impulso,/
Y abrasado en angustias criminales,/ Su corazón por la virtud
suspira").[45]

Meléndez' picture of a totally despairing man is precisely what
all the Byrons, Mussets, and Esproncedas were to portray years
later in the nineteenth century. As we look at the following verses
from Meléndez' elegy, we must remember two very significant
things. First, Meléndez provides a term in the Spanish language
for an emotional and "artistic" state long before such terms existed in other European languages. (English does not yet have a
designation.) And, second, Meléndez simply by employing the

term advances the early development of Spanish Romanticism
and emphasizes his primary position in that advancement:

> I see nothing, I find nothing that causes me
> But sharp pain or bitter boredom.
> Nature, in her varied beauty,
> Seems to my view to wrap herself
> In sad mourning, and, her laws being broken,
> Everything precipitates itself into the Antique chaos.
> Yes, my friend, yes: my soul, insensitive
> To the soft impression of vigorous pleasure,
> Darkens everything in its own sadness,
> Finding a source in everything for more grief
> And for this *fastidio universal* for which my heart
> Encounters in everything a perennial cause.

> *(Nada miro, nada hallo que me cause*
> *Sino agudo dolor o tedio amargo.*
> *Naturaleza, en su hermosura varia,*
> *Parece que a mi vista en luto triste*
> *Se envuelve umbría, y que sus leyes rotas,*
> *Todo se precipita al caos antiguo.*
> *Sí, amigo, sí: mi espíritu, insensible*
> *Del vivaz gozo a la impresión suave,*
> *Todo lo anubla en su tristeza oscura,*
> *Materia en todo a más dolor hallando,*
> *Y a este fastidio universal que encuentra*
> *En todo el corazón perenne causa.)* [46]

CHAPTER 4

Humanitarianism, Politics, and Poetry

I *Friendship*

MANY of the ideas and attitudes that we shall examine here are similar in tone to some we saw in Chapter 3, but we shall be especially concerned now with the more humanitarian aspect of Meléndez' poetry. This aspect includes many of his ideas responsible for some of the actions of his real, physical life. These actions, while the poet may not have considered them necessarily so himself, were at times tremendously political in tone. We shall not look at the poems, however, to understand specific events surrounding their creation, but with the simple intent of examining the attitudes they exhibit. This "political" poetry, along with the *Discursos forenses* (*Legal Discourses*) to be discussed in the last chapter, will round out our presentation of the man Meléndez was—a man of strong compassion, sensitivity, and love. These rather noble qualities are accompanied by the very human ones of ambition and pride. In no way will these latter disturb us, however. They will rather make us more fully understand the human warmth that Meléndez possessed and so eloquently expressed in the greater part of his total literary output.

We can begin our study with some paragraphs of the introduction to the 1820 edition. They were written not long after Meléndez entered his exile in France. As he looks at his present state of isolation and frustration, as he senses death approaching, he permits himself a very candid expression of his goals in writing poetry. The sincere tone that pervades this expression adds to its impact. The motivations for his work were not at all "political," as we see immediately. Preceding the date and place of writing— *Nîmes, en Francia, 16 de Octubre de 1815*—are the following significant statements:

I do not mean to imply that all the compositions are equal, just as in Virgil neither are all his eclogues nor all the books of his divine *Aeneid*, nor are all the odes of the pleasant, refined Horace, nor are all things men do really. Each thing has its proper merit and beauty the limits of which cannot be passed, and the author who realizes them reaches the edge of perfection. I did what my powers allowed, and then the years froze my inspiration and my enthusiasm. A lover of the Spanish muses, I have tried to dress them up with more taste and seasoning than I found in them and to make them speak the sublime language of ethics and philosophy [. . . .]

Young Spaniards, who love your country and its literature, it is up to you [. . .] to give our language and poetry the brilliance and majesty which they so rightly deserve [. . . .] Here you have a Pelayo, a Columbus, or the conquest of Granada for epic poetry—a genre which I once considered for myself [. . . .] Work, then, for your glory and your nation's, which go hand in hand [how succinctly he states his own purpose], and leave to me the lesser, but sweet and peaceful, glory of having begun almost without a guide, of having gone ahead among contradictions and calumnies, and of having achieved, at the end, with my own peace and fortune the innocent pleasure of renewing the sounds of the lyres of Garcilaso, Herrera, Villegas, and León.

But if in these sounds my readers find, through some fortune, only a bit of the peace and happiness that I have; if they inspire in them the innocent pleasures of the country, with all its tranquillity and simplicity; if my verses draw them away from ambition and greed and make them like their own situation, and kindle in their breasts the sacred enthusiasm and admiration for nature and love of country and virtue; if they imprint in young people the sentiments of good taste, the seeds of a cosmopolitan speech, the pleasant magic of language and the sweet longing for our muses [. . .] my hopes will be satisfied, my love for my country repaid, and my "efforts" will no longer have been merely efforts.

This collection could have been printed and published in France, and I would have been one of her writers interested in our language and literature, who today are many in reputation and interest. It was indeed proposed to me and someone even advised me to do it. But as I am a Spaniard in my principles and desires, I wanted my country to have it as an offering of my love, the last fruits of the inspiration of one of her sons who, offering her all that he has ever been capable, wanted to praise her with the most illustrious credentials and deeds and, honored with her attention, never once said or did anything that might lessen or stain her glorious name.[1]

There is a good synopsis here of what Meléndez intended in writing all his poetry. He is quite aware of his aesthetic mission and accepts the direction that his muses took without regret for not performing in the more heroic poetic meters. His emphasis on the philosophical foundations of his work stresses our line of study in Chapter 3. Meléndez is also stressing certain more social, moral themes that we have only briefly mentioned. These themes are essentially humanitarian ones that were so prevalent in the eighteenth century. Rousseau has become for us their official spokesman. Actually these themes were developing concomitantly throughout Europe. Rousseau may have had some influence on Meléndez' humanitarian attitudes, but I believe generally they are his own. The two basic humanitarian themes we need to consider are that of friendship and that of virtue.

After reading not only Meléndez' poetry, but that of other members of the Salamancan School, one is impressed by the importance and ubiquitousness of the theme of friendship. Their poetry is essentially written by and for friends. The happiness and consolation that one receives from mutual friendship is emphasized at all times. Friendship to these poets was man's noblest passion, in essence an expression of Platonic love. It is perhaps a little difficult for us to understand fully such an attitude because of our somewhat Victorian views concerning the relation of love and sex, especially among members of the same sex. Ironically, our current frantic attempts to rid ourselves of guilt feelings do not provide much greater insight either. In the kind of friendship we are speaking of here in Meléndez' case, the expression of a tender regard for the friend is the basic note. It is passionate, yes, but devoid of sex because it is a spiritual love among souls.

The stress on youthful beauty is also a bit embarrassing to us in our twentieth-century Victorianism. The importance of youth, which is very apparent in this poetry, just as in Rococo art, is implicit generally in all the poets' expression of the theme of friendship. A sexual connotation is not present, however. The seeming paradox is neatly exemplified in Meléndez' poetic name. The name "Batilo" was derived from that of Bathylus, one of the intimate young friends of Anacreon. We should not infer from this that Meléndez was homosexual. The point is, rather, that he was open and loving with his friends to an extent that we today are often completely incapable of comprehending. The poetic name because of its origin, then, can imply sensuousness and earthly feelings. And Meléndez was indeed a sensuous person, particularly in his youth, but the name "Batilo" and the sensuous quality of many of Meléndez' references to friendship should not be misleading. Again, our twentieth-century outlook may inhibit our ready acceptance of the simplicity and innocence of this theme.

The desire for youth is not so much in itself a narcissistic expression as it is a craving for the warmth and closeness associated with youth. The wish to embrace one's friend, to melt into him, to experience his thoughts, and ultimately to comprehend him are all actually a revival of the Platonic image of reading another's soul. This mutual comprehension recalls the Platonic concept that perfect beings mirror the divine. The respect and rapport inherent in this belief are essential to all the poets of the Salamancan School. The ease with which they consulted and criticized each other about their work indicates how deeply ingrained the concept was in them.

That friendship did exist naturally among these poets did not prevent its emphases being changed over the years. Meléndez' poem written at Cadalso's death is an excellent example. It provides good evidence of the melancholy inherent in these poets' concept of friendship. Friendship, because it is after all enjoyed by humans, is subject to the same laws of nature as human beings —principally that of death. While Meléndez' grief is genuine at the loss of his friend, his expression also contains much self-pity. This note should not bother us, however, for it reminds us that these men suffered and were just as misled as we all are. The capacity for friendship, for mutual understanding and love, was really no greater then than now, we should realize. It was then just as much in danger of being obliterated by man's more selfish nature as it is today. If we recall Meléndez' rage in the poem against the world about him, really quite a selfish rage, we should be pleased because we realize he was no more successful than we in achieving something more ideal in this world. This somewhat cynical realization on our part is important in drawing us to the poetry and the feeling, quite vulnerable, behind it. The empathy we experience with Meléndez creates between us, writer and reader, a greater bond than he, the writer, perhaps ever had with any friend of his own. This theme of friendship which develops gradually into a kind of egocentrism and ultimately leads to the narcissism of Romantic love in the early nineteenth century has much significance for us in our study of Meléndez Valdés. It is yet another indication of his leadership in the development of early Spanish Romanticism. Still, the greatest significance for us today is the theme's ability to move us, to join us to the poet in a kind of ethereal companionship and love.

Two poems, quoted in Chapter 3, very succinctly explain Meléndez' attitude toward his friends. The theme of Platonic love is inherent in these poems. The following lines come from Idyll VII, appropriately entitled "To Friendship," and illustrate the chaste honesty peculiar to this theme:

Try, try the fragile,	(Probad, probad ansiosos
Fine sentiments	Los sentimientos finos
Of friendship, enjoying	De la amistad, gozando
Their benign warmth.	De su calor benigno.
For the nectar which the bee	Que el néctar que la abeja
Sucks with sweet force,	Liva con dulce pico,
In the flowery valley	En el florido valle,
Of the purple hyacinth	Del cárdeno jacinto,
Has no comparison	Comparación no tiene
With the divine sweetness	Con el dulzor divino
That two friends with	Que dos amigos gozan
Simple intention enjoy,	De corazón sencillo,
When sitting side by side	Cuando a la par sentados
With simple honesty	Con simple desaliño,
Whatever they hide in their hearts	Cuanto en su pecho esconden
Tell each other without witnesses.	Se dicen sin testigos.
Their souls expand	Sus almas se dilatan
Just as in April	Como en Abril florido
The carnation opens its leaves	Abre el clavel las hojas
To the morning sun.	Al rayo matutino.) [2]

The more self-pitying, egocentric side of the theme of friendship is evident in the following verses from Ode XXVII "On the Unfortunate Death of Colonel Don José Cadalso":

Now everything is dead; the hard hand
Of cruel death, that hand
Thirsty with blood
Which prostrates power, force, beauty,

[126]

Like the harsh wind on a fragile grain field,
Only content with sorrow and tears
Took him violently away
To her black home [. . . .]
Unhappy one! Against the irresistible blow
Of the infernal shell, your singular
Virtues, what good were they?
Your lofty breast, your invinciple spirit,
Your profound counsel, and your divine
Intelligence, which brought you such praise [. . . .]
I, a stranger on earth
To joy and peace, blaming the heavens,
Always bathed in sighs and tears,
Whether morning's light exiles
And black sunset encloses
Dark night, whether the day
Again puts out its last ray,
And the world is plummeted into cold darkness [. . . .]
I shall never, never end
My painful lament.[3]

II *Compassion*

A natural result of the theme of friendship is that of compassion. Meléndez' personality was such that it naturally exuded feeling for those in trouble, whether close friends or strangers. This very basic attribute of his character was noted in our first chapter, when quoting Navarrete about Meléndez' life as magistrate in Zaragoza. The theme comes out vividly in Meléndez' *Legal Discourses.* The expression of the theme is in many of his poems and is perhaps best developed in one of his epistles, Number IV, "A un ministro, sobre la beneficencia" ("To a Minister Concerning Beneficence"). This rather long poem, first published in the 1797 edition, praises a minister for his judicious, compassionate judgments, but its main importance is its explicit revelation of Meléndez' own compassionate spirit. He in the beginning is quite humble, consciously lowering himself before the wisdom of the person he is addressing. I think by now we realize that this humility is not a manifestation of weakness or sycophancy, but rather of the façade that Meléndez continually created around himself in his poems. While on the one hand he wants to appear distant and objective, on the other he is actually very much involved in what he is saying. This characteristic is blatantly evident in several of the first verses:

> How can my humble muse render
> The deserved appreciation [. . . .]
> No, my muse is not enough, and your simple,
> Modest probity flees from applause,
> Content only in doing good [. . . .] [4]

From the self-effacing stance taken above, he goes on to admonish his subject to take up the cause of the poor and helpless, to put himself in their place so he may fully understand their plight and be even more loving and giving. Meléndez' tone strikes us as being extremely personal as he identifies himself with the underprivileged and forgotten. We recall the words from Ode XXIV noted in Chapter 3, where he referred to himself as "Orphan, young, alone and helpless." The words of that moving passage here take on a more universal expression. When he tells the minister how he must act, we see Meléndez' sensitivity at work in an altruistic fashion. The strength, too, of his expression is not lost on us. We should immediately grasp the essential force and, even, the threat behind his words. This is the champion of the oppressed speaking out here, not some maudlin weakling:

> Friend, let your goodness be your reward [. . . .]
> May it sound in your ears
> Without ceasing, and, powerful,
> Carry out generous endeavors,
> Giving sustenance to the widow
> And to the young, helpless orphan [. . . .]
> Oh, let your sensitivity
> Put you among them! See their
> Troubled solitude, see their hands,
> Their innocent hands extended
> Toward you, their protector, their shadow;
> See their sad faces, and
> Understand the happiness which, when they look at you,
> Comforts their wounded hearts.[5]

Meléndez next addresses Beneficence directly in the most laudatory terms. From here throughout the rest of the poem we can see his inherent humanitarianism reach its most cogent poetic expression. Two sides of the poet become quite apparent. One is the idealistic attitude of the sensitive *ilustrado*. The other side is the fighter, the fervent reformer who will brook no interference with the real attainment of his ideals. The paradoxes expressed and implied in these two attitudes are nicely underlined when, immediately after his address to Beneficence, Meléndez turns again to his friend and, seemingly quite humble, says he has no real wish to enter his friend's world of possible political influence and corruption. His words are all the more ironically intriguing when we remember how he did, of course, enter that world in 1789 and suffered greatly for it:

> Oh, sweet, oh, celestial Beneficence!
> Virtue that includes all the virtues [. . .]
> Whose essence is goodness, from whose hands
> A thousand gifts continually come down to earth.
> Happy is he who can exercise your power,
> Stopping the tears of the afflicted,
> And raising the oppressed,
> Image on earth of our common Father!
> You, illustrious friend [the minister], know my desires;
> You, my love for a peaceful life,
> Where in placid rest and retreat,
> I enjoy the favor of benign Muses,
> Far from ambition and the deceitful
> Sea of pretensions [. . .] never once, however,
> Do I desire to see myself on the high peak
> Of favor, as you see yourself [. . . .]
> My breast was made
> To love and do good, and a crown
> It holds less dear than spreading beneficence.
> A thousand times be happy, for you can
> Dispense it with a long hand, and to the throne
> You make the voice of misery rise
> Enjoying every moment
> The intimate pleasure of knowing the unfortunate
> Look to you as to a common father.[6]

Meléndez goes into what the compassionate arbiter of the law must be like. At the basis of the enumerated qualities is a sensitive comprehension of the unfortunate and their problems. Any government official without the ability to understand fully the situation of the person judged has no reason whatever being a judge. Compassion must be at the heart of all legal decisions, Meléndez is quite forcefully saying:

It is not enough, no, to be just. The severe judge
Who, the iron rod raised always
Against crime, his face inexorable,
Never felt tearful compassion
Fill his frozen breast with confusion
On seeing the white face of a prisoner
And hearing the harsh sound of chains
Must be despised. The sad wise man,
Who engulfed in arid problems
So as not to afflict his insensitive spirit
Closes his eyes, and turns his back
To the unhappy one who cries out against his harshness,
Must be despised. Even more so must be
The bloody hero, who is pleased
Among the horrors of fatal wars—
The ugly deaths and sad laments,
The blood, dust, and sounding brass—
With a vain crown of laurel. The person who knows
How to cry with those who cry, to share
Their cruel fate, with his counsel
To take away their afflictions,
To show them friendship,
To draw them to his compassionate breast,
To seek them out, and for their protection
Occupy himself; this one alone
By all is loved; his memory
Runs with a thousand blessings among the people;
His glory shines immortal; on earth
He is the joy and honor, and the image
Of the Divine among men.[7]

To refuse human compassion is a crime, Meléndez continues, in the following quotation. It is our duty "to come out of ourselves" and extend our love. But we in general are loathe to do this. The most ferocious of beasts is kinder with his own than man is toward his fellowman. A certain underlying pessimism thus appears in the last verses:

To show oneself indifferent to misfortune,
Is to double it [. . . .]

[130]

> Only what man gives does he keep,
> And neither death nor fortune can take it away.
> Let us come out of ourselves; let us extend
> Our love to all, and supreme
> Happiness to live, from the high empyrean,
> Will come down to the earth full of anguish.
> Ah! How can it be that with a serene face
> Or with dry eyes can the rich look at
> The poor suffer? The fierce tiger,
> If it sees a tiger suffer, tenderly grieves;
> And man is insensitive to misery!
> And sleeping in luxury, forgets the poor! 8

At the end of his poem Meléndez calls upon the minister to
join him in living with their fellowman in peace and harmony.
He pictures a Utopian existence in which comradeship will reign
among nations and people. The Rousseauistic ideal of brotherhood, of the essential purity of man when he is not contaminated
by the rigors of his civilization, is what Meléndez is advocating
here. In essence, this ode is very much an emotional outpouring of
the Age of Sensibility. The poor, the afflicted, the wronged are
the innocent sufferers, we are told. It is up to us, the more fortunate, to extend sympathy and understanding. Working together,
both the wronged and the more fortunate can create a better
world than the existing one. The theme of friendship, essential
to personal virtue, leads to compassion which in turn carries all
mankind to that paradisiacal existence for which all feeling
eighteenth-century individuals longed:

> Our fleeting days, wise friend,
> With bitter laments, full of cares,
> Let us live like brothers. With the weight
> Of our hardships let us go
> Along the difficult path of life;
> Let us help each other; the one who suffers
> Let us take up his burden; an unfortunate man
> Is rightly deserving of our help [. . . .]
> Who must not continually
> Fear cruel misfortune,
> Dear friend? Who has lived until now
> Without knowing tears? A thousand ferocious
> Enemies spy on our days,

And man is born to die on this earth.
It is a sacred law to remedy evil
According to our relative power, and he whom at the top
God places in control is there
So the afflicted may find succor in him,
The poor protection, the deserving a guardian.
Continue, then, your generous enterprise,
Oh, gentle friend! Finish it, and may my words
Not be forgotten in the serious
Problems that come upon you day and night.
Just listen to your sensitive heart [. . . .] [9]

III   *Duty and Patriotism*

The themes already studied logically lead us to this one of
duty—duty to one's own self and to one's own country. In the
first chapter of this book, we saw the physical events of Meléndez'
life in some detail. Critics both then and since have attributed
some of his actions to moral weakness, lack of character, or,
according to the more outspoken, cowardice. We noted that
Meléndez' actions never stemmed from these reasons, certainly
never from moral or physical cowardice. Beginning with his
marriage in 1782, Meléndez acted quite purposefully from strong
convictions. He knew what he wanted and proceeded in a logical
way to achieve his goals. His definitive entrance into the field of
law in 1789 is a second serious indication of what he was like.
Fundamentally, like any intelligent human being, he was thinking
of his own preservation and advancement with these two moves
and all those that followed in the stormy remainder of his life.
Again, as we noted in Chapter 1, and have just seen more fully,
there was another fundamental urge behind his actions—that of
love and compassion for his fellow sufferers in this world. I think
that we have been so negatively affected by so many really trite
summations of Meléndez that we have been unable to accept
him either as a strong individual, a masculine individual as it
were, or as a feeling participant in both the Enlightenment and
the Age of Sensibility, the latter period, of course, being the real
beginning of the Romantic period. We must once and for all
accept the fact that Meléndez was both—a man of personal drives
of all sorts, and a man of tremendous love for his brothers on this
earth. The next poem we shall look at will show us Meléndez'

commitment to the sense of duty that is implicit in such a realistic-idealistic individual.

The sense of duty was obvious in the poem just analyzed regarding compassion. Meléndez' belief in the necessity for this human quality best comes out in those poems where his national pride is most evident. Whether it is to bewail the state of the nation at some moment of peril, or to rejoice in some accomplishment of national renown, his idea is at all times the same: the mother country must be maintained in all her pride. A man can be whole only so long as his country is, he asserts. This spirit of ardent nationalism is not unexpected, surely, in Spain's first Romantic poet. Nor is it unexpected in a man who was also Neoclassic in much of his outlook. One has only to think of the ardent nationalism of an Iriarte or a Jovellanos, Spanish Neo-classicists to the core, to realize this.

Meléndez' most emotional nationalism is expressed in his two "Alarmas" ("Alarms") to the Spanish people after the French invasion of 1808. The poet's innocence manifested in the first poem is particularly touching. Like all Spaniards of the day, he had no idea that Ferdinand, the "victim" of the first strophe, was to make many of his countrymen victims of his ruthlessly conservative rule after 1813. The resultant poignancy of the beginning lines creates a certain mellow nostalgia in us today. To the people of his day the poem had more the effect of a ringing call to arms and we have earlier noted how this poem may have actually had some effect on the popular uprising in Madrid on May 2, 1808:

> To arms, to arms, Spaniards,
> For our good king Ferdinand,
> Victim of perfidy,
> Sighs, a slave in France.
> In his innocent goodness,
> For truth the flattery
> Of a treacherous friend he believed
> And ran unarmed into his embrace.
> Oh, if the ardent cries
> Of so many faithful vassals
> He might hear! Neither would he lament,
> Nor I call you to avenge him.
> But he was young and good,

And in his honorable heart
He discounted as impossible
Suspicions of double-dealing.
He was a king, grandson of kings;
As such, he held as sacrosanct
The guaranty offered him
By another king, his ally.
This guaranty, Spaniards,
Which even among inhuman savages
Was firm, always inviolable,
Only to a good king has been lacking.[10]

In the following verses Meléndez, in the voice of a "faithful Valencian" who is haranguing his audience, calls upon his compatriots to save their country from the ignominious situation created by Napoleon. He is very much like the old Spanish heroes he mentions—fierce, honest, faithful to a sense of common brotherhood:

To arms, to arms, Spaniards;
Your country calls you; let us run
To arm ourselves to avenge her,
Or as good men let us die [. . . .]
See [. . .] sad Italy [. . . .]
See the suffering Dutchman,
The Prussian, the rude Polack,
The noble German; of blood
All Europe is made a lake.
The blind Portuguese believed
His [Napoleon's] double promises, and his cities
Being sacked,
He is now cursing his mistake.
Because of the ambition of one man alone
The world suffers; the fields,
The factories, diligent
Industry, all destroyed.
We shall be what they are,
Vile, miserable slaves [. . . .]
These laws and this worship
Which we value so much,
In which we are born happy,
Which we absorb with our first milk,
Will end just as one day

> There in the times
> Of Witiza and Roderick
> They unhappily ended.
> And will they suffer it,
> The grandchildren of those who for eight hundred years
> Fighting against the Moor,
> Finally forced them back to Africa?
> And those who put up a heroic front
> To the invincible Roman,
> And with Saguntum and Numancia
> Burned themselves up, indomitable?
> No, such cowardice does not fit
> In the Spanish breast; let us turn
> Our eyes to our ancestors
> And take care to imitate them.
> An army is nothing
> Against a people who, joined
> In a faithful knot, its homes
> Defends against another bold agressor.
> Ten million Spaniards
> Are not, not wanting to be, slaves [. . . .] [11]

The "Second Alarm" is directed to the Spanish army and, coming shortly after the first one when the political situation was even more dangerous, is much more personal. The poet is very upset at the negative atmosphere of the moment. His call is frenetically, passionately patriotic in the final lines:

> [The tyrant] is coming, and the cities burn,
> As if a torrent of lava
> Were covering them up, and the earth
> Is inundated in human blood.
> No, soldiers! No, Spaniards!
> No, good Lord! Such infamy
> And impious abomination
> Shall not befall us.
> Run, sons of glory,
> Run, the trumpet calls you
> To save our homes,
> Religion and country.
> May the lazy be reviled
> Just as he who turns his back.
> I myself, spirited, follow you,

And shall oppose the cannon with my breast.
Let us go forth, for God guides us,
Since the cause is His [. . . .] 12

In another poem he speaks of his country with the love of a
son toward his mother. The deeply-felt affection, respect, and
love are strong here. They are sincerely experienced emotions
and could not in any way have come from a weak, ambivalent,
traitorous individual. The narrator in this ode, Number XXVIII
(written after May, 1814), is a pilgrim who has been long away
from his homeland. The fact that the words are spoken by
another person is a subtle device, seen in the poem quoted above,
that merely heightens the personal, autobiographical effect of
the poet's words. The poem is entitled "Afectos y deseos de un
español al volver a su patria" ("Emotions and Desires Felt by a
Spaniard on Returning to His Homeland"):

Benign, at last the heavens
Heard my sighs; the day
That my heart so impatiently
Desired breaks forth brilliantly,
For I prayed so very fervently [. . . .]
Oh, sweet country! whose holy name
Today is confused in my happiness
With soft crying
That consumes me, if I sing your praises [. . . .]
You opened, mother earth,
Your heart at last to your sorrowing children,
Who in eternal orphanhood,
After such evils,
Were mourning, their eyes always fixed on you [. . . .]
All united in one,
All in holy peace, all brothers,
Divisions now far away,
Far away vain men,
Who stirred up such insane ill-will [. . . .] 13

IV Politics

Even though we have seen certain of Meléndez' basic beliefs
only in brief, we can nevertheless understand how the tenor and
expression of these beliefs may have caused problems for the
poet, particularly in the chaotic period in Spain after the French

Revolution. His motivations, especially the humanitarian ones, are those of the truly enlightened individual of the eighteenth century. At one time in Spain, before the death of Charles III in 1788, Meléndez might have fared well in acting on his beliefs. When he did enter the real judicial world, it was already too late to escape the personal chaos that political confusion on national and international levels would bring him. In Chapter 1, some attention was paid to what conflicts he encountered after his abrupt change of life style in 1789.

Again we must emphasize that Meléndez knew quite well what he was doing. However, the consequences of some of his unfortunate political decisions were not always anticipated by him. Such a failure to estimate the political climate about him is intriguing. On the one hand, it shows a dedication of the poet-jurist to his ideals and a more or less conscious disregard of what the results might be. On the other hand, it shows his inherent faith in mankind, his refusal to believe the worst in others, his desire to better man's life, and finally a sort of persevering ingenuousness on his part. This last characteristic, too, is greatly responsible for many of his critics' attacks on him for his supposed moral weakness. It is actually the critics who are at fault for not comprehending his essential idealism. Still, it is fascinating that Meléndez, a subtle, intelligent man, could allow himself to become enmeshed in some of the political difficulties that did engulf him. The constant interplay of political sagacity and naïve sensitivity is one of his most appealing attributes.

Many of his poems blatantly manifest his political objectives, while some are more subtle. The quotation to follow is from his first discourse written in 1787 and entitled "La despedida del anciano" ("The Old Man's Farewell"). It is principally a monologue by a patriotic old gentleman exiled from his country by "hatred and envy." He expresses great disillusionment with his times and the government's inabilities to take care of all its people. Avarice especially has so corrupted the nation's nominal leaders that they are unable to respond to the difficulties. The poem is of interest to us because it comes only two years before Meléndez' entrance into the legal field where he would attempt to remedy the ills he found around himself. Also, it pictures certain conditions in Spain at the end of the reign of Charles III, Spain's most enlightened ruler. Meléndez' open address to the King below in its honesty and bluntness shows us the poet's most conscientious attitude toward his country's leaders:

> Where is that Castilian honesty,
> The moderation, the simple
> Faith, that among all peoples
> Distinguished the Spanish [. . .]?
> But today everything has changed:
> The desolated cities
> Cry for their nobility,
> They call for their noblemen,
> While these latter at court,
> With games, banquets, and women,
> Spend the gold of their estates
> With blind frenzy;
> And the poor farmer
> Crying over his small harvest of grain
> Watches the wheat that a steward of his lord
> Takes away from him [. . . .]
> Oh, just Charles! To your throne
> His cries do not reach?
> Oh, vile interest! you alone are,
> You, the cause of so many evils [. . . .]
> But you, corrupt century [. . .]
> Your teaching is this? This the
> Fruit of all your wisdom [. . .]? [14]

Meléndez' concern over governmental strictures and the government's lack of interest in the arts and sciences is quite visible in the first epistle written in 1795 and included in the 1797 edition of his poems. It evidences the same sort of apprehension about the nation's state seen in the first discourse. Addressed to Manuel Godoy, it shows no sycophancy for which Meléndez has at times been blamed in his relations with this minister. If anything, his attitude here is more that of counselor to the Prime Minister:

> Even more than protector, be the firm shield
> Of those who follow, prince, the steps [of art. . . .]
> The pleasing rain, the liquid dew,
> All work for the common good,
> And show the power of the great Being.
> Thus a wise minister seeks the universal good

> Of his people who in turn trust
> In his wisdom and provident kindness.
> He directs all his actions to this good [. . . .]
> While the people he rules, fortunate,
> Acclaim him father [. . . .] [15]

Epistle XI, written in 1797, was also directed to Godoy. The language is much more abrupt, and the attitude is severely questioning. There is no intimation of sycophancy here either. Even when we recall that the 1797 edition of Meléndez' poetry was dedicated to Godoy, it is difficult to find anything in this poem but an intense cry of alarm at the present political situation. Godoy even quotes from the poem in his *Memoires* to show how much he was maligned and suffered at the hands of his political enemies during this period: "So that no one will say I am exaggerating . . . and to show how much the general public knew the torments my enemies caused me I copy below as an historical document a brief selection from the *Epistle on Calumny* that Juan Meléndez Valdés addressed to me at that time." [16] Meléndez writes:

> In the silence of night, when
> In deep calm the world
> Lies under its dark blanket,
> Flee disturbed from my sad eyes,
> Sire, placid dreams pursued
> By the horrible monster of calumny [. . . .]
> I see, sire, in vague clouds
> Your spirit weaken; the cries
> Of error I hear [. . . .] [17]

In his study of Meléndez, Georges Demerson includes two poems dedicated to Joseph I. The first one, written in 1810, is a sincere outpouring of feeling from the poet overwhelmed by a generous act of kindness on the King's part. Joseph, while making a triumphal tour of Seville, was approached by a child recently orphaned. The King publicly ordered that he be admitted to a school in the city where he would be cared for. Meléndez immediately composed his "Oda al rey nuestro señor" ("Ode to the King Our Lord") on April 20, 1810. His tone is one of admiration for the new King. There is no intentional political stance taken here, however. We find, rather, a simple outpouring of feeling not unexpected under the circumstances: "Continue, oh well beloved/ By Heaven, with open arms/ Doing good and alleviating sorrow;/ And never, even one day, will you have lost." [18]

Meléndez wrote a poem in July, 1811, on Joseph's return from Paris. It is much longer and not so adulatory as the preceding one. Certain events, such as the annexation of some Spanish provinces by Napoleon, were perhaps on his mind. Demerson also notes the many changes that Meléndez made in the poem before it was published, indicating there may have been some outside influence on his attitude. Nevertheless, in the final version he is blunt in what he says, demonstrating his love of justice and desire for a peaceful, happy homeland seen in the preceding quotations. The tone is therefore of necessity somewhat more "political." For us its real value lies in its forceful portrayal of the poet, striving as always to maintain a dignity and honor for his country and his countrymen. We are at the heart of Meléndez *afrancesado* here. Quite ironically, and significantly in the light of later criticism for his supposed *afrancesamiento*, he turns out to be only a man who loved his homeland very much.

The protagonist in the poem is Spain herself. Addressing Joseph, she reiterates the horrors of war all about her, the blindness of her sons, and her hopes for salvation through the King's efforts:

> Come, my son, my protection and hope;
> Run and save the lacerated remains
> Of my former grandeur [. . . .]
> Be pleased at the people's contentment:
> But observe around you closely
> And your own happiness will cease.
> How I regret upsetting you with my cares!
> From my fields destructive rage
> Robbed their verdure.
> The plowshare was forged into an unholy sword.
> See the fire of my arts burned out,
> And my factories burned and deserted;
> And in my safe ports
> My strong ships destroyed by Britain [. . . .]
> Come to me and dry my tears [. . . .] [19]

[140]

The anguish his country feels is, of course, Meléndez' own and is even more evident in the last two poems to be considered. The first is Number XXIX of the *Philosophical and Sacred Odes* entitled "A mi patria en sus discordias civiles" ("To My Country in Her Civil Discords"). It was written sometime between 1809 and 1813. The emotions are no different from those in the second ode to Joseph, although alarm for the present and future of Spain and horror at the chaos throughout the country are emphasized. Since the poem is from the Napoleonic period, its continuing expression of Meléndez' attitudes seen since 1787 makes the odes addressed to Joseph seem all the less sycophantic. The poet's anguish no doubt stems from the ineffectiveness of his humanitarian love in bringing about universal brotherhood. The anguish is all the more poignant because the poet is old and sees his world falling apart around him. All he has fought for in his life is literally in disarray:

> When will heaven
> Give you peace, oh my country!
> And, the odious scepter
> Of unholy discord broken,
> When will happiness return to your august breast [. . .]?
> Oh, may the happy day dawn,
> Oh, may it dawn finally when glorious peace
> May embrace you, oh my country;
> Into delightful calm
> May the heavens turn your ominous anger;
> And in your love burning,
> As your sons at your feet we shall prostrate ourselves;
> All errors forgotten,
> Let us love like brothers
> And rest happily on your sweet breast.[20]

The poignancy of Meléndez' situation exhibited above is heightened and climaxed in his Ballad XXXIX, "El náufrago" ("The Shipwrecked Man"). The poem was written in 1814. He now feels the heartbreak of exile that will accompany him to the grave in 1817. The futility of all his hopes, beliefs, and actions weighs heavily on his mind. He senses that his judicial career, his "politics," have brought him to this low point. He is old, frail, and despairing, and he fully realizes that the end of his life is inevitably near. Yet for us today the picture he paints becomes more than just that of a defeated old man, for we are led to recall him on earlier occasions. We remember the happy, young Rococo artist, the enlightened, sensitive philosopher, and the humanitarian judge. We the readers feel for him the love, understanding, and compassion that he himself felt for others and expressed in his poems. Meléndez experiences with us, then, years later, the realization of his hopes and beliefs enumerated in this chapter. It is unfortunate only that he himself could not see his success:

> When, inconstant fortune,
> Will you stop pursuing me,
> Nor my unhappy heart be a target
> For your shots? [. . . .]
> My eyes, just as a magnet
> Is directed to its pole,
> Turn toward Spain,
> And still, deceived, pretend to see her [. . . .]
> Thus only with hopes
> Does my wounded heart still live.
> Not for one brief instant
> Do I forget you, Spain.
> Sweet homeland [. . .]!
> Your love boils in my veins [. . . .]
> Imperious necessity
> Took me from you [. . . .]
> When, when, my country,
> Shall I happy
> Embrace you and render
> The noble homage of my love?
> I shall render it, yes, and with your name
> My name shall stand,
> And with your life my life
> Forever shall be identified [. . . .]

> (*¿Cuándo, inconstante fortuna,*
> *Dejarás de perseguirme,*
> *Ni será blanco a tus tiros*
> *Mi corazón infelice?* [. . . .]
> *Mis ojos, bien como al polo*
> *Fijo el imán se dirige,*
> *Así hacia España se vuelven,*

Y aun verla ilusos se fingen.
Así de esperanzas sólo
Mi llagado pecho vive
Sin que haya ni un breve instante
Que de tí, España, me olvide.
¡Dulce patria [. . .]!
Tu amor en mis venas hierve [. . . .]
Necesidad imperiosa
Me echó de tí [. . . .]
¡Cuándo, cuándo, patria mía,
Lograré feliz decirte:
Ya te abrazo; el noble feudo,
Grata, de mi amor admite!
Admítelo, y con tu nombre
Mi nombre orgulloso brille,
Y con tu vida mi vida
Por siempre se identifique [. . . .]) [21]

CHAPTER 5

The Discursos forenses

I *Man and Society*

THE *Discursos forenses* (*Legal Discourses*), published in 1821, one year after the four-volume edition of Meléndez' poetry, may be considered a fifth volume of his general works. We have left the *Discourses* to be discussed last for several reasons. They are first of all in prose, being for the most part legal treatises written around 1798 when Meléndez was District Attorney of Madrid. Even more important, their overall tone is extremely humanitarian and patriotic and thus they follow very nicely the discussion in Chapter 4. Further, because of their humanitarianism, the *Discourses* portray more of Meléndez' Romantic spirit for us. The essential nature of Romanticism is not really its interest in the historical, literary past, but its humanitarian concern with the unfortunate and the oppressed. Significantly for our own purposes, Romantic altruism in Spanish literature is very well exemplified in Meléndez, particularly in these essays, and emphasizes once again his importance as the father of Spanish Romanticism.

Noting the volume's contents briefly and quoting rather extensively, we shall complete the picture of Meléndez as a kind, loving man whose interest in others was the greatest guiding force in his life. A statement at the end of the editor's introduction to the *Discourses* shows this altruistic characteristic of Meléndez' personality very simply. It is interesting to see how after Meléndez' death and his obvious exit from politics a critic, when he wanted, could be impartial in his judgments of the poet's actions. The editor is speaking of the last essay in the volume which concerns beggars and the threat they posed in various ways to the country. The essay was dedicated to an official who succeeded in placing ten children for whom Meléndez had been caring in a philanthropic institution. The editor understands Meléndez' so-called politicking very well when he notes the selfless reasons for this essay: "[. . .] Meléndez took advantage of his relations with illustrious people of his time. Almost all the compositions he directed to them, particularly in flattering verses, revealed to them important truths and energetic lessons that he could never have told them otherwise." [1]

The first of the discourses concerns the prosecution of two people on trial for murder. A wife and her lover were accused of having murdered her husband. It was a particularly scandalous and popular trial because of the love triangle and the husband's relative prominence. Meléndez gave this speech before the court on March 28, 1798. The wife is portrayed as the very opposite of what the ideal wife should be. The lover's portrayal is no less unpleasant. Meléndez almost gets carried away in his disgust and horror at the pair. He relates the death scene with exquisite Romantic intensity and melodrama, for example. Only a scene from *Don Álvaro* could provide suspense and exaggeration comparable to that developed in the following lines:

Permit me to take you now in your minds to that bedroom, sad theater of desolation and evil, so that you will cry and be shaken by the scene of blood and horror that is played out there. A good man in the flower of his life and filled with the most noble hopes, attacked and killed within his own house, unarmed, naked, rolling in his blood, thrown from the conjugal bed by the very one who caused it to be stained. Consider that he is wounded in his very bed, the surest and most sacred refuge of man. He is surrounded by his family in his death agony without anyone's being able to help him. While he calls for his wife, this fury, this monster, this unholy woman turns her back on the patricide and pretends to faint so that her treacherous lover can escape [. . . .] [2]

While the Romantic flavor of this description is important for our examination, Meléndez himself is most concerned with the crime itself. For Meléndez its implications for mankind and civilization are so horrible that he graphically imparts to us his horror. Among his closing lines the ones quoted below illustrate his concern for the concept of family and for human warmth, love, and mutual assurance. He feels that these basic foundations of any society are thoroughly threatened by this crime:

[The murderer] attacks personal security in its most intimate and sacred part. He attacks the holy conjugal knot and impiously breaks and destroys it. He attacks public custom and all that is right and venerable on this earth. With this fatal example before us, who will trust anybody? Who will be able to open his heart to gentle friendship if his friend conceivably will kill him? Who will be kind or generous if his reward is death? Who will be able to sleep calmly in his bed if while in it and surrounded by family and servants poor Francisco Castillo was not safe? [3]

The next essay is a prosecuting speech given on April 23, 1798, against a man accused of having murdered his wife. Whereas in the first case he was markedly opposed to any clemency being shown the accused, in this case he is much more merciful. He takes up for the husband. It must be said that the husband's situation sounds very much like that of the more fortunate young husband in Don Juan Manuel's short story about the ferocious young woman who could not be tamed. Perhaps the greatest misfortune of Meléndez' criminal was that he did not have a dog, cat, or horse on which to first demonstrate his temper. Meléndez' description of the couple is enlightening in its illustration of his fairness: "He is a man whom María [the wife] herself considered crazy. She held him in no esteem, telling everyone she saw just what she thought of him. He was a man joined to a hardheaded, capricious woman who had been separated from him for six months. In spite of everything he loved her tenderly and tried in every way to please her. In short, he was joined to a woman who was like a scourge to him in every way." [4]

After calling for punishment of the accused but still asking for clemency, he writes the following paragraph to conclude his case. It is one of the most feeling, lyrical cries in these essays. We see the same kind, gentle man that we have seen throughout his poetry:

How unhappy I would be if I did not have this relief and sad release among the thorns of my bitter work! If I could not cry and be touched by the very unfortunate people I have to accuse and pursue. How very, very unhappy I would be if I had to talk without remembering gentle reasonableness, stifling in my breast the sweet sentiments of commiseration and indulgence which make me consider as my own the misfortunes of my brothers and associate me intimately with all their troubles and miseries.[5]

The third discourse is his prosecuting summation in a case against a man accused of incest with his daughter. The father had abandoned the child when she was little, but returned when she was about thirteen years old. At the time of the trial (the date of this speech is May 21, 1798) the girl is seventeen and the father, thirty-seven. The daughter is only lightly condemned. Meléndez reserves the strongest words for the father whom he pictures as the devil incarnate defying the laws of God and man. In all fairness, Meléndez does point out that incest was an accepted and honored practice among the "Persians, Medes [. . .] and other peoples of antiquity," but they were deceived and blinded by "the laws and practices of their false religions." [6] As in the first case, Meléndez is upset by the horror he sees in the crime, but he is even more concerned by the implications the crime has for the future of mankind. In some of his statements we find a good combination of the enlightened intellectual and the sensitive soul, those two characteristic personalities of the eighteenth century that Meléndez so well personifies for us.

The beginning sentences of this essay show what I mean very well. On the one hand we find implied the hopes for the betterment of man, the essence of the enlightened attitude of the period, and on the other we find expressed the sad realization that such a desired goal is unattainable because of the very nature of man himself. Bitterness and disillusion, Romantic emotions really, are what most affect us as we read the opening lines:

How certain it is that man, this prodigious being, so vain because of the dignity of his nature, and so proud and satisfied because of his preeminence and enlightened mind, is nevertheless nothing more than an abyss of misery and sad corruption, worse than beasts themselves when he abandons himself to the fury of his passions! And how truthfully it is said that, no matter how much one studies man whether as a social group or as an isolated individual, one can never know ultimately what man is! Neither books nor the greatest philosophers' teachings can tell us, no matter how detailed and complete they are! [7]

The violence that Meléndez feels toward a man whose passions have led him into a most abject state is obvious in the following

lines. As in some other instances, Meléndez does not appear at
all impersonal in his condemnation of those who allow passion to
overwhelm reason: "Unhappy man! A thousand times unhappy!
Nothing is pleasant to your eyes but darkness, nor to your heart
but crime. Nothing arouses your pleasure but what leads you to
the most lamentable perdition. For you, honesty and virtue have
lost their celestial grace, the consolation of sensitive souls. Their
immaculate purity no longer shines in your eyes." [8]

Toward the end, when he builds up to a climactic indictment of
the incestuous pair, Meléndez describes what would happen
were the concept of family as we know it to be substituted for
one in which incestuous promiscuity were permitted. The corner-
stone of civilization would be removed, he believes. It is significant
to note that the man speaking here is Rousseauistic in his basic
nature, but that he is also logical enough to emphasize the
happiness, duties, and hardships of a way of life that in all its
imperfections he much admires. This is again Meléndez at his
best—a feeling, compassionate friend of man but a harsh judge
of anyone who would threaten the stability of man's existence
with his fellowman. If the families should lose their sense of
morality, then they, those "sweet refuges where peace exists in
the heart of good order, where innocence and virtue lodge,
where the worries of the soul can calm themselves [. . .] would
consume themselves in furious anger [. . . .] Suspicion would
succeed kind, simple trust. The affection that unites sons, father,
and brothers would disappear. In its place would come lasting
hatreds and vengeance, the mere thought of which makes us
tremble." [9]

The next speech concerns a man accused of having stolen
jewels from a statue of the Virgin of Almudena. The date is
June 14, 1798. Meléndez wishes no mercy shown the accused.
When excuses are made for his conduct within the church—that
he fell asleep and, rather than awake anyone, remained there
until morning, Meléndez loses all restraint. It was during this
time he supposedly stole the jewels, Meléndez reminds the judge.
He then goes into a rather sarcastic diatribe against the suspect
and those who would excuse him. I include Meléndez' words
here because they show us the morally incensed, righteous, almost vindictive side of our poet:

He remained asleep in the church and woke up about ten o'clock at night. And at that hour, what with the fear that merely being alone there should have caused, he was nevertheless so in possession of his faculties that he determined to remain there and quietly await the dawn, supposedly so as not to arouse suspicion. Strange resolution indeed! It is an odd compliance in a married man with children anxiously awaiting him at home and with a good wife calling him there who would be upset precisely because of his delay. The very fact that he did not escape until morning condemns him of the suspicion he says he tried to avoid! Certainly, my Lord, anyone in his place would be less suspicious yelling until he awoke someone than waiting in silence the entire night to avoid being seen.[10]

Meléndez wants full punishment as much for the public good as for the moral uplifting of the individual accused. Throughout this particular speech, Meléndez is very upset over the degeneration of society's morals. He sees the present affront to the Church as the height of indecency which slowly is creeping over the Spanish mentality in general, or so he fears. For this reason, he asks the judge at the end for a severe punishment to warn the populace of its errors. Meléndez, without realizing it, appears very much like an Old Testament prophet seeking to return his people to the chosen way. This quality that Meléndez takes on in his legal career adds a new, more poignant dimension to his stature as a literary artist and philosopher. In the following lines he addresses the judge very forthrightly:

As the pure voice of the law, impose your just decision on the unfortunate Manuel C . . . *as a lesson for this city* [italics mine . . . .] Let all learn from his sad head that churches are inviolable; that the religion which occupies them covers and defends them; that the city must be safe; that those who would assault her safety will pay for their acts with their lives; and that finally you, your Worship, although you may be moved in your soul and compassion may be called for, have no other guide or immutable rule in your decisions than the holy laws you swore to on beginning your august duties.[11]

His veiled admonitions to the judge not to be swayed by emotions or compassion for the individual involved are an amusing addition. Whether from personal knowledge of the judge or simply the desire to see justice done as he thinks fit, the important thing for us is to note the limitations Meléndez would place on humanitarian feelings. Meléndez wants love and understanding to be extended to his fellowman, yes. But he does not want them extended unthinkingly. Where there is reason for deserved punishment, he realizes that one cannot be swayed by misguided altruism or some sort of maudlin sentimentality. I do not think we can ever emphasize this point too much in Meléndez' case because when we do, we negate once more any criticism of weakness or cowardice that may be directed against him and the actions of his public life.

The variety of the discourses' contents is astounding. The essay following the accusation of the jewel thief concerns a cattle thief. Meléndez considers this crime, too, a heinous one and refers to laws from Antiquity to the present to sustain his views. At one point he lets his hopes for the betterment of mankind carry him off in idealized fantasy. To show the thread of humanitarian ideals that guides him throughout these legal treatises, I include the next quotation. Although his words start out as an exposition of the culprits' evil doings, by now they have become an impassioned plea against permissiveness. Underneath, too, they are a cry of disillusion at the imperfectibility of man. We find once more the enlightened person of the eighteenth century foiled by that very being, man, whom he would praise to the skies and consider totally infallible:

The man who knows how to elevate himself by his virtue and great deeds almost to the perfection of an angel can also lower himself at times to a point lower than the grossest of beasts. Then, a slave and victim of his blindness and vices, he forgets honor, virtue, public decorum, saintly honesty, and even the most pleasing and sublime affections. In vain does an observant eye strive to find in him the original figure that distinguished him above the rest. His life becomes that of an animal, and his inclinations and acts those of a very evil one at that.[12]

At the end in his summation Meléndez sounds even more vitriolic in his attack, which perhaps is a bit difficult for us to understand. But we have only to remember the importance of cattle and horses in the everyday life of that period and indeed up to our own century. Giving himself a sound foundation in the *Siete Partidas* of the thirteenth century, Meléndez calls for a strong condemnation of the accused. Again we must note the importance attached to the benefit of mankind in general by so doing:

Take him, your Worship, from the company of honorable men since he cannot be one of them. Take him away for being a cattle thief and a totally lost vagabond because law six under the title *On Thieves* [from the *Siete Partidas*] requires it. Through the punishment of criminals public security and the well-being of innocence are maintained. Dead trees, weeds, parasitic and sterile plants should be pulled up and a diseased branch must be cut off. Thus, Sire, this man who because of his evil life, his criminal idleness, and abominable conduct has not been able to find one person who would dare to vouch for him certainly is not worthy of the society he lives in. Nor can he give us any hope that in the future he will be any better, returning by means of punishment to a wholesome life of honesty and work. Let him live and breathe far away from us then, he who like some disease can only infect us.[13]

II *Literature and Society*

The next discourse is against the printing and selling of popular ballads. Meléndez is not referring to those poems that deal with the exploits of heroes such as Pelayo or Guzmán the Good, but to those that tend to stir up the public for no good purpose. The ballads he is concerned with here are some " 'Coplas en alabanza de nuestra España de la guerra que ha comenzado' ('Verses in Praise of Spain in the War Begun' [With England]), seized from a blind man who was selling them in the streets. You, your Worship, ordered them brought in, their author ascertained, and established where and with what license they have been printed." [14]

It is not just these verses he is concerned with, however:

What should merit your attention if you wish to use it wisely today, as I heartily beg you in the name of literature, morals, and public customs, is [. . .] to penetrate deeply into the grave evils that this type of writing causes among the people. In this way you will cut off the error at its very roots. In time, with a legislative resolution, these indecent ballads that are printed and spread about so freely to the discredit of our nation and its culture will be banned once and for all. It certainly would serve no good purpose to gather up the verses I am speaking about if your Worship leaves the way open for others just as ridiculous and even more gross and immoral.[15]

The tone of this particular essay is slightly different from that of the others. Principally it is one of horror at the ignorance existing in a nation that likes to consider itself civilized. The tone, then, is that of the pure *ilustrado*, but with a slightly new twist—one of patience and sadness. Meléndez realizes he cannot rid the Spanish mentality of empty, banal interests with frenetic efforts. Once again his concern about a problem and his manner of resolving it recall attitudes of Tomás de Iriarte. The profound similarities of these two enlightened Spaniards really are much more noticeable than any of their superficial differences. Iriarte wrote a work in the late 1780's that criticized many of the same things Meléndez criticizes here. The only difference in their approach to the subject is a superficial one once more. Iriarte, deadly serious in his intention, wrote in a humorous vein.[16] Meléndez was rarely able to write biting satire and does not attempt it here. He instead stoically and somewhat bitterly writes against these foolish poems. Quite succinctly, in the lines below, he is the disillusioned but patient *ilustrado* who ultimately realizes that man cannot be perfect. He does not use humor to cover up his real emotion and he does not turn to despair, which many a later Romantic will do when confronted with the same problem. In miniature we have a very good picture of Meléndez here— the steady fighter against at times insurmountable odds:

These poems, shameful relics of our old slang and abortions rather than productions of starving necessity and crass ignorance [. . .] provide nothing for good taste or sound reason which might free them from the ban I ask for [. . . .] They are either ridiculous little stories of supposed miracles and vain devotions [. . .] that endanger the mind from infancy onward with false and harmful ideas about the most holy aspects of religion and its mysteries [. . .] or they present indecent narrations which offend both the modesty and decency of the public. They corrupt one's soul and heart and leave in one without realizing it indelible impressions whose ill-fated results were never foreseen at the beginning [. . . .] [17]

Meléndez defends his position by giving a short history of poetry and pointing out that such vulgar trash as the court is here concerned with does not even approach the realm of poetry. He expresses the Neoclassic facet of his mentality while emphasizing the sublime moral and aesthetic heights of poetry:

Poetry and song are of all times and always entered the most august institutions, the most celebrated legislators making use of them as a powerful means for calming rebellious spirits. In verse [. . .] the precepts of morality, the healthful laws of matrimony, and the laws that governed all actions and contracts were given to the first men. In verse were sung simple as well as heroic deeds. The martial spirits of men were inspired by poetry. Man's first histories were written in verse. And there was nothing great which was not sung about in divine poetry, believed then, I do not know whether correctly so or not, to be an inspiration from Heaven and consecrated, as it should be, to scattering with its gallant flowers the narrow path that leads to virtue so as to make it less harsh for man. Let us try to follow such useful examples as much as possible. Imitating wise Antiquity, let us return this sublime art to its first noble principles [. . . .] [18]

Instead of the vapid poems he is condemning, he would have Spaniards read and hear of the noble deeds of their ancestors. After all, what other nation has such a glorious store of heroes? In them Spaniards will admire "the heroic love of country, invincible constancy, austere probity, the ardor of work, gravity in deeds and words, modesty, frugality, and the other virtues which were a part of those great men, in whom valor was a habit and rectitude a necessity, and which contrast so poorly with the vileness, the disorder, and effeminacy of our day." [19]

As he continues, Meléndez sounds more and more lyrically idealistic. The serious concern he shows throughout the volume is not really lost now, however. Meléndez, the man, is simply carried away into a sort of ethereal philosophizing. In a way this is his manner of escaping the too harsh reality of the particular situation just as Iriarte's sardonic humor was his way, but Meléndez does not rhapsadize so as merely not to face the unpleasant situation. In the next quotation he sees himself as simply doing his job, both the real task of ridding the public of such trash and that of elevating its outlook to a higher level. Meléndez the enlightened crusader is at work with all his sensitive, idealistic forces preparing the way for him: "Let us paint with simple, brilliant colors the delights of private life. Let us celebrate the professions that adorn society and animate and enrich it at the same time. Let us offer consolation to all states and make them aware of the happiness at hand of which they are perhaps unaware. In this way, scattering the bitter road of life with flowers and sympathy, shall we make men exist in peace, loving their station in life." [20]

III Courts of Justice

The next essay concerns the González-Luquede affair we discussed in Chapter 1. As we pointed out then, the case is significant in proving Meléndez' attitude toward Church and State. The court system of the latter should have precedence is his idea as he urges the Church to return to its more spiritual functions. Demerson points out that this decision occurred in the reign of Joseph I, as we note in Chapter 1, and not under Charles IV as the editor of the *Discourses* implies.[12]

The next discourse was given on April 27, 1791, at the opening of the new court of justice in Extremadura. Meléndez is full of hopes on this great day because it signifies a new life for this province he so greatly loves. He starts off in a lofty tone, saying that one ordinarily would expect to hear praise of the King (Charles III) who saw the need for such a court or of his successor (Charles IV) who sees the court established today. He does praise them indirectly, of course, and then states what he will talk about—the good of the people that can be achieved through this court:

The brief repository of my talents and eloquence must confess itself very inferior to such a difficult task [that of praising the Kings] and leaves it willingly to a greater master of celebrating virtuous and great deeds. As I am joined with you by our profession [. . .] I would like to speak to you about [. . .] the obligations we take on our shoulders from this signal day forward and about the rigid necessity of carrying out these obligations imposed on us by honor, gratefulness, and all that is sacred in man. We must not defraud the public who watches us in silence [. . . .] [22]

After these thoughts, which fit in quite nicely with the general theme throughout the volume of humanitarian good will, Meléndez presents other ideas. A principal one concerns the laws of the country. He repeatedly cites the need for keeping the laws abreast of changing social conditions. His wish that laws reflect human needs is quite urgent in tone and emphasizes once more for us the modernity of Meléndez' social awareness: "Criminal law, even though less imperfect than in other nations, is still not free among us of fatal errors [. . . .]Oh, if our glorious vigils could in time make the delinquent's situation in prison less severe! If they could make his arrest without the risk of escape less common! If they could abbreviate and simplify the proofs in his defense and in his sentence! If they could narrow the wide gap between offense and punishment! [. . . .] If among so many laws that punish him they could only write one that would reward a man for his virtue [. . . !]" [23]

The very open attitude seen here continues to manifest itself throughout the essay. One thing we must remember is that Meléndez is addressing a very educated audience, one he hopes will seriously consider what he says. Even though his desires, in essence, are what we have come to expect in all his work by now, we can understand, too, that he is expressing himself formally and vulnerably to a public that could denounce him or cause him trouble if it so desired. The fearlessness with which the ideas in this speech are enumerated is striking indeed. Meléndez does not fear recriminations or criticism. He is carried away by his desire for that Utopian world he has always wanted to exist in reality. The candor and the resultant vulnerability should greatly intrigue us therefore. The man speaking to us is not some frightened, cowering individual threatened by his circumstances. This is a man who speaks out against wrongs and injustices, who proposes, even though at times in an idealistic language, a realistic re-evaluation of man's circumstances as he sees them.

The following quotation shows how very blunt he can be. He calls for reform of civil law in the most assured terms: "Our law codes are an arsenal where all may find arms for their particular desires and pretensions. They are like the King's armories where old pieces covered with rust and centuries-old dust are found all together. The codes contain contradicting laws, some laws with no determined purpose, and insufficient and useless laws amended over the years. They contain everything except unity and organization, everything except principle and a general objective." [24]

Meléndez soon goes into areas less accurately defined. He begins to outline, according to his criteria, the reasons for the present state of lawlessness in Spain. This is a theme that appears frequently in this volume of essays. Meléndez' tone cannot be considered reactionary, although this might be the initial impression we receive. He is upset at the breakdown of what he feels were solid bases for society. The seeming lack of limits is disturbing to his organized mind. It is because he thinks new definitions are needed that he has called for a reevaluation of civil law noted above. He continues the same feelings in the lines below, but what principally intrigues us is the rather quixotic attitude underlying his desire for change. His words have even more pertinence for us today because of the tremendous similarity to what we hear preached to us about our own country and our own time. The fascinating comparison between what he saw occurring or having occurred in Spain and what has occurred in our own national dilemmas recently draws us closer and closer in intimacy with Meléndez:

Our forefathers, simple in all their actions, soldiers more than citizens and dedicated to war and agriculture, were content with little and knew few real wants and themselves appeared in the law courts and defended their causes. Good faith served them as a lawyer, and the judge was rather a pacific arbiter of their differences than the severe minister of the law who decided these differences according to the law. Society went along "perfecting" itself, however [. . . . And all the accompanying evils became more and more evident in the courts], and then a dark web wove itself over the august simplicity of the law making a shameful business of justice, filling her sacrosanct temple with a starving swarm of people interested only in obfuscating court transaction in order to enrich themselves at the expense of ignorant credulity.[25]

The tone of this quotation is reminiscent of Don Quixote's speech on the Golden Age. We noted earlier this same tone in a poem of Meléndez. Whether there is a direct influence here or not, one cannot be certain. Nevertheless, just as with Cervantes and Don Quixote, the disillusion so peculiar to the cynical idealist, if we may be permitted once more this seeming contradiction, does appear here. The comparison between a past time—whether it be in the past of one's country or in some idealized sphere that never really existed—and the present with all its too detestable reality is natural to any idealist who is incapable of completely accepting the real world as it is. Usually such an idealist does nothing to try and remedy the evils about him, content merely to criticize them. In Meléndez' case this was not so, of course. To some degree, nevertheless, the inherent idealism he possessed, with its companions cynicism and disillusion, made it difficult for him to see real change come about through his efforts. One wonders, for example, how much he actually expected to see the idealized future of Extremadura he portrays below and how much of what he says was purely poetic fabrication. Yet whatever the real strength of these fabrications was, they were necessary for Meléndez if he was to continue being a poet, a jurist, or simply a man:

Today the opportunity has been given to us of realizing this salutary desire for the general good of Extremadura. Let us look at this province for a moment [. . .] new in everything, permit me to say, and entrusted to our hands. Wherever we look we can pull up a vice and sow a virtue. How small is her population! [. . . .] Wild country and frightful thickets occupy precious, extensive land which cries out to us for cultivation in order to prove its natural fertility and to feed thousands of new inhabitants. Her fertile valleys and plains await irrigation from the rivers which now harm instead of enriching them [. . . .] What grand, sublime objectives for our zealous concern that can provide happiness for 450,000 souls who now turn to us! 450,000 souls, gentlemen, 450,000 souls are waiting for their happiness from us. Look at them surround us, fix their eyes on us, bless this day as one of complete justice and the culmination of their hopes, and with acclamations and tears cry out to us: "Ministers of justice, unite in your judgments both humanity and justice. Close your ears to appeals for denunciations and accompanying vengeance and divisions of families. It is better for certain to forget an excess than to open this awesome door to calumny and involve an innocent man in the cruel doubts of a judgment. Consider as your own the sacred honor of the family, for you must understand that you govern an honorable, generous people [. . . .] [26]

IV *Poverty and Welfare*

The last selection in the *Legal Discourses* is entitled "Fragmentos de un discurso sobre la mendiguez" ("Fragments of a Discourse on Beggary"), written probably in 1802 and dedicated, as we noted at the beginning of this chapter, to a minister thanking him for his help in placing ten orphans Meléndez had befriended. The *Fragments* have several significant ideas in them very much in tune with those we have seen so far in this volume of legal opinions. The main concerns in this essay are government welfare, the need for human dignity provided by work and not government relief, and the necessity for setting up an organization to aid the poor—the main idea being to help them when they help themselves.

Meléndez' attitude is extremely personal as it has been in most all the discourses. The tone is set from the very first lines when he indirectly refers to his exile that had come about in 1798 as a result of personal animosities from certain government officials (see our Chapter 1). He begins:

My intention here is not to examine the present state of our poorhouses or their imperfections and reforms [. . . .] The government has given this duty to a board of zealous, illustrious people who will carry it out properly with *facts that I do not have in my retirement* [italics mine]. But neither can I fail to observe even in passing that these worthwhile establishments erected in different times by different people with different ideas and principles do not have among themselves the least system of organization that they should have for effective, fruitful results [. . . .] [27]

He goes on to discuss the evils that beggary has for both the individuals involved and the society of which they are a part. He distinguishes quite vividly between the wealth of part of the citizenry and the abject poverty the beggars exhibit. Pointing to the severity of Antiquity toward beggars, he urges the Spanish government to energetic action against them. He would have the giving of alms by Church and private individuals stopped because it only generates further indolence. Unless all individuals realize the necessity for work, for mental and physical occupation, there will be no end to the situation as it exists. He writes: "Let us realize that not to contribute to the society in which we live with a return share of work for the subsistence and aid it gives us is to laden unjustly the working class, to overwhelm it with this new weight, and robbing it of its time and labor to live ignominiously by its sweat. And finally to feed a beggar because of some misplaced compassion is the same thing in the eyes of reason, as paying a salary to some malefactor who lives at the expense of the victims he despoils [. . . .]" [28]

Continuing his ideas on the need for all people to work and produce, Meléndez gives us some excellent statements in brief of his philosophy of life. The concept of productivity is inherent in all people, he affirms. It manifests itself in different ways but it is nevertheless there. It is up to the government, an enlightened one obviously, to see that this productivity is brought about for the good of society as a whole:

Emulation in the arts and sciences is, among exalted souls who desire glory, what profit, the desire to acquire, or even the spirit of greed in the mechanical arts, the tilling of the fields, and other common exercises are among the general masses [. . . .] Society needs the first no less than the second set of motives in order to enrich itself [. . . .] What is important for morality and government is to direct both passions well. The salutary desire to distinguish oneself and be famous must not become an empty ambition to dominate what ultimately is only corpses and ruins. In short, the spirit of acquisition and covetousness must not degenerate into an exclusively sordid, vile passion that subjugates the heart and absorbs all its sentiments and affections.[29]

Meléndez' last major point deals with the establishment of an association that would take care of the needy. His ideas are those of the perfect eighteenth-century *ilustrado* imbued with a Rousseauistic sensitivity inherent in the Romantic mentality. The modernity of what he says is again striking. Perhaps it would be fairer to Meléndez and others of his day to say that we have little improved on the eighteenth-century enlightened methods proposed here by Meléndez. Our inability also emphasizes the basic timelessness and humanitarianism essential to these methods:

I believe that only a charitable association can carry out the important job of caring for the poor [. . .] an association that is authorized by the most illustrious faction in the capital [. . .] and the best people in the lowliest of towns. It would be an organization decorated with civil honors and sanctified with the Church's approbation [. . . . Among the association's principal functions would be] the listing and classifying of the poor and needy of the provinces [. . .] the distribution of alms to all according to their needs [. . .] the establishment of a method for this distribution [. . .] the bringing together of all beggars and vagabonds on one specified day in order to disperse them among various charitable institutions or return them to their native villages [. . .] to carry out the same action in regard to orphans [. . .] to provide work for them and prohibit forever afterward beggary and vagrancy with the severest punishments [. . .] to prohibit with the same severity all public almsgiving in the street since it produces only more idleness [. . .] and finally to interest public opinion in this great undertaking. And how many more objectives could such an association not undertake [. . .]? Would it be far-fetched for it to send these beggars into the country to till the fields? Could the government not lend its aid in establishing these unfortunate people in the many underpopulated areas we have? Could not these people plant the many thousands of trees we need and assure the harvest with irrigation [. . .]? [30]

Much of this essay's tone is found in the poem it inspired, Epistle X. The expected lyrical idealism is naturally more notable. At first Meléndez thanks the minister for having helped the ten orphans, and further on he calls for the stringent measures toward beggars that he asks for in the discourse. He cries out at the end with that patriotic fervor seen in Chapter 4 at the failure of Spain to deal with her poor as forthrightly as England. The lyricism of the poem nevertheless is essentially what attracts us. One strophe in particular cogently sums up what he says in the discourse:

> Far from vile opprobrium, from bitter complaint,
> From torpid idleness and its evil effects,
> In the sweat that will flood their brows,
> And with the wages earned by their own hands,
> Industry blessing them with its gifts,
> They will free themselves,
> And men will be men—and citizens.[31]

V Conclusion

The end of this chapter brings us to the conclusion of our book. The subject matter and tone of the *Legal Discourses* have provided a good final stamp to our portrayal of Meléndez. His deeply felt concern for his fellowman and his almost fanatical resolve to protect the structure of man's society emphasize once and for all the inherently humanitarian outlook that the poet maintained throughout his lifetime. His Romantic concept of the world in these essays nicely accentuates his position as the first

Romantic literary artist in Spain. At this point we can look back at the themes of each chapter which were gradually leading us to this sweeping statement.

In the first chapter we saw both the joyous and troubled nature of Meléndez and how he was affected by this nature as well as by events beyond his own real control. The picture we saw was of a man who acted from strong convictions of what was right and wrong. Even though the events themselves in his life at times seemed to deny a cohesive line of action, we nevertheless always found Meléndez acting from a sensitive, enlightened, and positive point of view. The second chapter, in its denial of certain criticisms formerly made of Meléndez' "lighter" poetry, denies just as well what at first may seem a certain superficiality in his life. My assertion that artificiality is not necessarily existent in most of his work stresses the profundity that lies beneath not only his work, but beneath his total personality. The third chapter's tracing of the basic philosophy at work in his poetry points up Meléndez' comprehension and eventual advancement of literary technique in the eighteenth century. His synthesis of different philosophical directions into a dynamic new vision marks the beginning of Romanticism in Spain. This very early manifestation of that literary movement declares Meléndez its originator long before its existence in the 1830's. The fourth chapter defines the humanitarian outlook in Meléndez' poetry and illustrates his open participation in the eighteenth-century Age of Sensibility. In addition, it shows the reasons for many of his political difficulties in the last half of his life.

The emphasis of the present chapter on Meléndez' Rousseauistic humanitarianism in his prose brings us to our last, very positive statements about him. His work, sometimes unjustly maligned in the past, is significant in its representation of the ever-changing philosophical and artistic viewpoints of the eighteenth century. It therefore enables us to understand a very basic period in the development of modern man's thought and underscores Meléndez' importance in the evolution of modern Spanish literature. And finally, his life, lived in accordance with the dictates of his humanitarian philosophy, provides us with a brilliant example of the richness of the Spanish eighteenth-century experience.

Notes and References

Chapter One

1. Emilio Cotarelo y Mori, *Iriarte y su época* (Madrid: Est. Tipográfico "Sucesores de Rivadeneyra," 1897), p. 227.

2. Georges Demerson, *Don Juan Meléndez Valdés Et Son Temps (1754–1817)* (Paris: Librairie C. Klincksieck, 1962), p. 5. Demerson lists five children at Meléndez' birth and another born two years later. However, he himself believes his list incomplete.

3. *Ibid.*, p. 9.

4. *Ibid.*, p. 13.

5. *Ibid.*, p. 14, quoting Martín Fernández Navarrete's unedited *Noticia de la vida y escritos de don Juan Meléndez Valdés.* Here also, and on pp. 4–5, Demerson gives the source for the name *Valdés.*

6. Manuel José Quintana, *Noticia histórica y literaria de Meléndez*, *BAE*, 19 (Madrid: Imprenta y Estereotipía de M. Rivadeneyra, 1852), 109.

7. Juan Meléndez Valdés, *BAE*, 63 (Madrid: Ediciones Atlas, 1952), 80. (This particular printing of Vol. 63 is the one referred to hereafter.)

8. Raymond Foulché-Delbosc, "Obras inéditas de don José Cadalso," *Revue Hispanique*, 1 (1894), 324.

9. Meléndez Valdés, *BAE*, 61 (Madrid: Ediciones Atlas, 1952), cvi–cvii. (This particular printing of Vol. 61 is the one referred to hereafter.) The date of Cadalso's death is definitively established in Russell P. Sebold's "¿Qué día murió Cadalso?" *Hispanic Review*, 40 (1972), 212–15.

10. Demerson, p. 24.

11. M. Serrano y Sanz, "Poesías y cartas inéditas de D. Juan Meléndez Valdés," *Revue Hispanique*, 4 (1897), 303–04.

12. *Ibid.*, 305.

13. *Ibid.*, 306–07.

14. Meléndez Valdés, *BAE*, 63, 76.

15. William E. Colford, *Juan Meléndez Valdés*, (New York: Hispanic Institute, 1942), p. 91.

16. Meléndez Valdés, *BAE*, 63, 76–77.
17. *Ibid.*, 77.
18. Demerson, p. 24.
19. Meléndez Valdés, *BAE*, 63, 78–79.
20. Demerson, p. 25.
21. Joseph de Viera y Clavijo, *Elogio de Felipe V* (Madrid: Joachin Ibarra, 1779), pp. 1–2.
22. For more specific and complete information on the polemic, the reader may want to consult Cotarelo, my own *Tomás de Iriarte* (New York: Twayne Publishers, Inc., 1972), or José Jurado, "Repercusiones del pleito con Iriarte en la obra literaria de Forner," *Thesaurus*, 24 (mayo-agosto de 1969), 228–77.
23. Colford, p. 96.
24. *Ibid.*, p. 97 and Demerson, p. 26.
25. Ramón de Mesonero Romanos, *Memorias de un setentón* in *Obras*, 7 (Madrid: Renacimiento, 1926), 134–35.
26. Quintana, 112.
27. Demerson, p. 99. The author searched out the original *licencia* and includes it on pp. 98–99.
28. *Ibid.*, pp. 99–100.
29. José Somoza, extract from his *Una mirada en redondo a los setenta y dos años*, *BAE*, 61, cxxxviii.
30. Demerson, p. 104.
31. Colford, p. 347. This is a previously unedited letter written on August 13, 1782.
32. Demerson, pp. 113–14, quoting from A[rchivos de la] U[niveridad de] S[alamanca], libro 242, 4 de julio de 1783 and AUS, libro 243, 24 de marzo de 1784.
33. George H. Addy, *The Enlightenment in the University of Salamanca* (Durham: Duke University Press, 1966), pp. 178–79, quoting from AUS, libro de claustros, 1783–1784, Junta de Derechos, 21 de mayo de 1784.
34. *Ibid.*, p. 114, quoting from AUS, libro 244, 18 de noviembre de 1786.
35. See my *Tomás de Iriarte*, pp. 50–52.
36. Demerson, p. 116.
37. For further information see Demerson, pp. 117–19.
38. *Ibid.*, p. 122.
39. *Ibid.*, p. 133.
40. Juan Sempere y Guarinos, *Ensayo de una biblioteca española de los mejores escritores del reynado de Carlos III*, 4 (Madrid: Imprenta Real, 1787), 59.
41. *Ibid.*, 60.
42. Serrano y Sanz, 309.

43. Demerson, pp. 137–43.
44. *Ibid.*, pp. 146, 447–50. See also Russell P. Sebold, *El rapto de la mente: poética y poesía dieciochescas* (Madrid: Editorial Prensa Española, 1970), pp. 257–64.
45. Demerson, p. 148.
46. *Ibid.*, p. 156.
47. *Ibid.*, p. 161, quoting from Martín Fernández Navarrete.
48. Rafael Altamira, *Historia de España y de la civilización española*, 4 (Barcelona: J. Gili, 1914), 332–33.
49. Demerson, p. 199.
50. *Ibid.*, p. 205.
51. Colford, p. 115.
52. Demerson, pp. 211–12, quoting Navarrete.
53. Colford, p. 117.
54. *Ibid.*, pp. 117–23.
55. Charles E. Chapman, *A History of Spain* (New York: The Mac-Millan Company, 1918), pp. 407–10.
56. It is interesting to note that it was in this same part of the Peninsula that the Reconquest began in 711 under Pelayo.
57. For further information on the Oviedo affair, the reader may want to see Colford, pp. 126–28 and Demerson, pp. 261–78.
58. Michael Glover, *Legacy of Glory* (New York: Charles Scribners' Sons, 1971), p. 94.
59. Demerson, pp. 291–95.
60. *Ibid.*, pp. 353–57.
61. *Ibid.*, p. 363.
62. Quintana, 119.
63. Demerson, p. 419, quoting a letter to Doña María's nephew, Benito de la Riva y Coca.
64. Colford, pp. 133–36.

Chapter Two

1. For more information on the literary tenets of Tomás de Iriarte, the reader is referred to my *Tomás de Iriarte* or Russell P. Sebold, *El rapto de la mente*, pp. 141–96.
2. Meléndez Valdés, *BAE*, 63, 93a.
3. Meléndez Valdés, *Poesías*, 1 (Madrid: Joachin Ibarra, 1785), vi.
4. *Ibid.*, ix.
5. *Ibid.*, x.
6. The reader may wish to consult a new study for more facts about Anacreon and the homosexual attitude in Arno Karlen's *Sexuality and Homosexuality* (New York: W. W. Norton and Co., Inc., 1971).
7. Meléndez Valdés, *BAE*, 63, 93a, b.

8. *Ibid.*
9. E. Allison Peers, ed., *A Critical Anthology of Spanish Verse* (Berkeley and Los Angeles: University of California Press, 1950), pp. 318–19.
10. Meléndez Valdés, *BAE*, 63, 94c.
11. *Ibid.*, 95b, c; 96a.
12. Antonio Machado, *Poesías completas* (Buenos Aires: Editorial Losada, 1958), p. 81.
13. Meléndez Valdés, *BAE*, 63, 96a.
14. *Ibid.*, 96a, b.
15. *Ibid.*, 99c, 100a.
16. *Ibid.*, 100a.
17. *Ibid.*, 102a.
18. Raymond Foulché-Delbosc, "*Los besos de amor*, odas inéditas de don Juan Meléndez Valdés," *Revue Hispanique*, 1 (1894), 76, 77, 81.
19. Meléndez Valdés, *BAE*, 63, 125b, c.
20. George Gordon, Lord Byron, *The Poetical Works of Lord Byron* (London: John Murray, 1876), p. 468.
21. Meléndez Valdés, *BAE*, 63, 125a.
22. *Ibid.*, 127b.
23. *Ibid.*, 128a.
24. *Ibid.*, 131a, b.
25. *Ibid.*, 140a.
26. *Ibid.*, 147a.
27. *Ibid.*
28. *Ibid.*, 147b.
29. *Ibid.*, 147b, c.
30. *Ibid.*, 156a, b.
31. *Ibid.*, 159a.
32. *Ibid.*, 161a.
33. Alfred Cobban, ed., *The Eighteenth Century: Europe in the Age of Enlightenment* (New York, St. Louis, San Francisco: McGraw-Hill Book Company, 1969), p. 232.
34. Meléndez Valdés, *BAE*, 63, 176b.
35. *Ibid.*, 177a.
36. *Ibid.*, 177b.
37. *Ibid.*, 178b.
38. *Ibid.*, 149b.
39. *Ibid.*, 149c.
40. *Ibid.*, 150a.

Notes and References

Chapter Three

1. José Mor de Fuentes, *La Serafina* [1797], ed. Ildefonso-Manuel Gil (Zaragoza, 1959), p. 113.

2. J. C. L. Simonde De Sismondi, *Historical View of the Literature of the South of Europe,* trans. Thomas Roscoe, 2 (London: George Bell and Sons, 1883), 428.

3. Russell P. Sebold, *El rapto de la mente,* pp. 57–97.

4. *Ibid.,* pp. 194–95.

5. Ignacio de Luzán, *La poética o reglas de la poesía,* ed. Luigi de Filippo, 1 (Barcelona: Selecciones Bibliófilas, 1956), 57–60. See also I. L. McClelland, *Ignacio de Luzán* (New York: Twayne Publishers, Inc., 1973).

6. Russell P. Sebold, "Enlightenment Philosophy and the Emergence of Spanish Romanticism," *The Ibero-American Enlightenment,* ed. A. Owen Aldridge (Urbana: University of Illinois Press, 1971), p. 118.

7. John Locke, *An Essay Concerning Human Understanding,* ed. A. D. Woozley (Cleveland and New York: Meridian Books, The World Publishing Co., 1969), pp. 211–12.

8. *Ibid.,* p. 213.

9. Etienne Bonnot de Condillac, *Traité Des Sensations* in *Oeuvres Philosophiques,* ed. Georges Le Roy, 1 (Paris: Presses Universitaires De France, 1947), 222, 248.

10. *Ibid.,* 305.

11. Alexander Pope, *An Essay on Man* in *The Complete Poetical Works* (Boston: Houghton Mifflin Co., 1931), p. 140.

12. *Ibid.,* pp. 141–42.

13. Pope, *An Essay on Criticism* in *The Complete Poetical Works,* pp. 68–69.

14. See Demerson, pp. 61–78, for an alphabetical catalogue of Meléndez' library.

15. Meléndez Valdés, *BAE,* 63, 73.

16. Azorín [pseud.], José Martínez Ruiz, *De Granada a Castelar* in *Obras completas,* 4 (Madrid: Aguilar, 1948), 352–53.

17. *Ibid.,* 354.

18. *Ibid.,* 357.

19. Meléndez Valdés, *BAE,* 63, 99a, 100c.

20. *Ibid.,* 93c. A comparison of the original verses of Meléndez and Machado is in order here:

> *¡Oh! ¡cómo en tus cristales,*
> *Fuentecilla risueña,*
> *Mi espíritu se goza,*
> *Mis ojos se embelesan!*   (Meléndez)

The exuberance of these lines should not prevent our understanding

an inherent melancholy which is more openly expressed in the lines of
Machado below:

> El limonero lánguido suspende
> Una pálida rama polvorienta,
> Sobre el encanto de la fuente limpia,
> Y allá en el fondo sueñan
> Los frutos de oro [. . . .]   (Antonio Machado, p. 23)

21. Meléndez Valdés, *BAE*, 63, 259b.

22. *Ibid.*, 260a.

23. *Ibid.*

24. *Ibid.*, 262b. The quotation from Blake is from *William Blake,
A Selection of Poems and Letters*, ed. J. Bronowski (Baltimore: Penguin Books, 1964), p. 67. The date of Meléndez' poem is provided by
Demerson, p. 587.

25. Meléndez Valdés, *BAE*, 63, 217a, 218a.

26. *Ibid.*, 218a.

27. Manuel Godoy, *Memorias*, *BAE*, 88 (Madrid: Ediciones Atlas,
1956), 234–35.

28. Meléndez Valdés, *BAE*, 63, 235a, b; 236a.

29. *Ibid.*, 230b.

30. *Ibid.*, 231a, b.

31. *Ibid.*, 227a.

32. *Ibid.*, 229a, b.

33. *Ibid.*, 223a.

34. *Ibid.*, 224a. Compare the beginning lines of this strophe to those
of "A Felipe Ruiz":

> ¿Cuándo el día será, luciente y puro,
> Que en suave soledad contigo unido,
> El ánimo cuidoso
> Pueda enjugar sus lágrimas seguro [. . .]? (Meléndez)

> ¿Cuándo será que pueda
> Libre de esta prisión volar al cielo,
> Felipe, y en la rueda
> Que huye más del suelo,
> Contemplar la verdad pura sin duelo? (Fray Luis de León in
> Peers, p. 214)

35. Meléndez Valdés, *BAE*, 63, 225a.

36. *Ibid.*, 239a, b.

37. *Ibid.*, 198a, b.

38. *Ibid.*, 252b, 253b.

39. *Ibid.*, 130b.

40. *Ibid.*, 131c.

41. *Ibid.*, 193a.

42. *Ibid.*, 193b.

43. Russell P. Sebold, *El rapto de la mente,* pp. 123–37. Sebold has also shown that the first occurrence of this attitude, although unnamed, is in a poem by José Cadalso, "A la muerte de Filis," published in 1773. See his "Enlightenment Philosophy and the Emergence of Spanish Romanticism," pp. 130–31.
44. Meléndez Valdés, *BAE,* 63, 250a.
45. *Ibid.,* 251a.
46. *Ibid.,* 250.

Chapter Four

1. Meléndez Valdés, *BAE,* 63, 91–92.
2. *Ibid.,* 131a, b.
3. *Ibid.,* 239b, 240a.
4. *Ibid.,* 202b.
5. *Ibid.,* 202b, 203a.
6. *Ibid.,* 203a.
7. *Ibid.*
8. *Ibid.,* 203a, b.
9. *Ibid.,* 203b.
10. *Ibid.,* 158a.
11. *Ibid.,* 158b.
12. *Ibid.,* 159c.
13. *Ibid.,* 240a, b.
14. *Ibid.,* 256a, b; 257a.
15. *Ibid.,* 200a, b.
16. Godoy, 245–46.
17. Meléndez Valdés, *BAE,* 63, 213a, b.
18. Demerson, p. 318.
19. *Ibid.,* pp. 325, 327.
20. Meléndez Valdés, *BAE,* 63, 241a, 242a.
21. *Ibid.,* 153a, c; 154a.

Chapter Five

1. Meléndez Valdés, *Discursos forenses* (Madrid: Imprenta Real, 1821), p. vi.
2. *Ibid.,* pp. 13–14.
3. *Ibid.,* p. 39.
4. *Ibid.,* p. 61.
5. *Ibid.,* p. 70.
6. *Ibid.* p. 72.
7. *Ibid.* p. 71.
8. *Ibid.,* p. 83.
9. *Ibid.,* p. 98.
10. *Ibid.,* p. 123.

11. *Ibid.*, pp. 149–50.
12. *Ibid.*, p. 153.
13. *Ibid.*, pp. 165–66.
14. *Ibid.*, p. 168.
15. *Ibid.*, pp. 169–70.
16. See my *Tomás de Iriarte*, pp. 48–49.
17. Meléndez Valdés, *Discursos forenses*, pp. 170–71.
18. *Ibid.*, pp. 174–75.
19. *Ibid.*, p. 176.
20. *Ibid.*
21. Demerson, p. 291.
22. Meléndez Valdés, *Discursos forenses*, p. 232.
23. *Ibid.*, pp. 249–50.
24. *Ibid.*, p. 261.
25. *Ibid.*, pp. 262–63.
26. *Ibid.*, pp. 265–67.
27. *Ibid.*, pp. 273–74.
28. *Ibid.*, p. 284.
29.. *Ibid.*, pp. 290–92.
30. *Ibid.*, pp. 296–98, 300–301.
31. Meléndez Valdés, *BAE*, 63, 212.

Selected Bibliography

PRIMARY SOURCES

Works by Meléndez Valdés

MELÉNDEZ VALDÉS, JUAN. *Poesías* (Madrid: Joachin Ibarra, 1785). First edition of Meléndez' poetry.
———. *Poesías.* 4 vols. (Madrid: Imprenta Nacional, 1820). First posthumous edition. Most complete to that time.
———. *Poesías. Biblioteca de Autores Españoles,* 63 (Madrid: Ediciones Atlas, 1952), 67–262. The most complete and most accessible edition to modern readers of Meléndez' poetry.
———. *Poesías,* ed. Pedro Salinas (Madrid: Espasa-Calpe, 1955). An easily obtained volume in the *Clásicos Castellanos* series. The introduction is rather superficial.
———. *Poesías inéditas,* ed. Antonio Rodríguez Moñino (Madrid: Real Academia Española, 1954). Provides some previously unedited material. Valuable for its indexes that give dates, etc.
———. *Discursos forenses* (Madrid: Imprenta Real, 1821). See our Chapter 5.
(For more bibliographical information on Meléndez' own works the reader should consult Demerson or Colford: see below.)

SECONDARY SOURCES

Books and Articles
ADDY, GEORGE M. *The Enlightenment in the University of Salamanca* (Durham: Duke University Press, 1966). A penetrating study of the University in the eighteenth century.
ALBORG, JUAN LUIS. *Historia de la literatura española, siglo XVIII,* 3. 3 vols. (Madrid: Editorial Gredos, 1972). A new history of Spanish literature of this period containing many references to Meléndez.
ALTAMIRA Y CREVEA, RAFAEL. *Historia de España y de la Civilización española.* 4 vols. (Barcelona: J. Gili, 1900–1914). A study of Spanish history with penetrating ideas on the eighteenth century.
CHAPMAN, CHARLES E. *A History of Spain* (New York: The MacMillan Co., 1918). A very good study in English of Spanish history.

COBBAN, ALFRED, ed. *The Eighteenth Century: Europe in the Age of Enlightenment* (New York, St. Louis, San Francisco: McGraw-Hill Book Company, 1969). An excellent presentation of the arts and sciences of the eighteenth century. Beautiful photographs.

COLFORD, WILLIAM E. *Juan Meléndez Valdés* (New York: Hispanic Institute, 1942). The best general study of Meléndez in English.

COTARELO Y MORI, EMILIO. *Iriarte y su época* (Madrid: Est. Tipográfico "Sucesores de Rivadeneyra," 1897). A very complete study of Iriarte. It provides much detail about Meléndez and the eighteenth century in Spain as well.

COX, R. MERRITT. *Tomás de Iriarte* (New York: Twayne Publishers, Inc., 1972). A general study of Iriarte and his times.

CUETO, LEOPOLDO AUGUSTO DE. *Bosquejo histórico- crítico de la poesía castellana en el siglo XVIII, BAE,* 61 (Madrid: Ediciones Atlas, 1952). An early, comprehensive study of the Spanish eighteenth century.

DEMERSON, GEORGES. *Don Juan Meléndez Valdés et son Temps (1754–1817)* (Paris: Librairie C. Klincksieck, 1962). There is a Spanish translation: *Don Juan Meléndez Valdés y su tiempo (1754–1817).* 2 vols. (Madrid: Taurus Ediciones, 1971). The most authoritative and exhaustive study of Meléndez available.

FOULCHÉ-DELBOSC, RAYMOND. "*Los besos de amor,* odas inéditas de don Juan Meléndez Valdés," *Revue Hispanique,* 1 (1894), 73–83. See our Chapter 2.

———. "Obras inéditas de don José Cadalso," *Revue Hispanique,* 1 (1894), 258–328. Valuable to see Cadalso's relations with his close friends.

FROLDI, RINALDO. *Un poeta illuminista: Meléndez Valdés* (Milano, Varese: Istituto Editoriale Cisalpino, 1967). A synopsis of Meléndez' artistic formation.

GLOVER, MICHAEL. *Legacy of Glory* (New York: Charles Scribners' Sons, 1971). An investigation that provides sound, new ideas about the Bonaparte rule in Spain from 1808 to 1813.

GODOY, MANUEL. *Memorias, BAE,* 88, 89 (Madrid: Ediciones Atlas, 1956). Interesting for its personal tone from a man who was in the midst of the national difficulties in Spain from about 1790 to 1808.

HERR, RICHARD. *The Eighteenth-Century Revolution in Spain* (Princeton: Princeton University Press, 1969). Contains several important references to Meléndez.

JURETSCHKE, HANS. *Los afrancesados en la guerra de independencia. Su génesis, desarrollo y consecuencias históricas* (Madrid: Ediciones Rialp, S.A., 1962). Provides new light on the Bonaparte period. A good companion to Glover's work.

Selected Bibliography

LUZÁN, IGNACIO DE. *La poética o reglas de la poesía,* ed. Luigi de Filippo. 2 vols. (Barcelona: Selecciones Bibliófilas, 1956). A limited, twentieth-century edition of Luzán's work.

McCLELLAND, I. L. *Ignacio de Luzán* (New York: Twayne Publishers, Inc., 1973). A general study of Luzán.

MESONERO ROMANOS, RAMÓN DE. *Memorias de un setentón,* 7–8 of his *Obras.* 8 vols. (Madrid: Renacimiento, 1926). A costumbristic document of the nineteenth century that has references to Meléndez.

POLT, JOHN H. R. *Gaspar Melchor de Jovellanos* (New York: Twayne Publishers, Inc., 1971). A general study of Jovellanos.

QUINTANA, MANUEL JOSÉ. *Noticia histórica y literaria de Meléndez, BAE,* 19 (Madrid: Imprenta y Estereotipía de M. Rivadeneyra, 1852). A valuable early biography of Meléndez.

SARRAILH, JEAN. *L'Espagne Éclairée De La Seconde Moitié Du XVIII Siècle* (Paris: Imprimerie Nationale, 1954). A very good cultural, sociological, political study of the period.

SEBOLD, RUSSELL P. *Colonel Don José Cadalso* (New York: Twayne Publishers, Inc., 1971). A general study of Cadalso.

————. *El rapto de la mente: poética y poesía dieciochescas* (Madrid: Editorial Prensa Española, 1970). Excellent series of articles on various literary subjects of the Spanish eighteenth century.

————. "Enlightenment Philosophy and the Emergence of Spanish Romanticism," *The Ibero-American Enlightenment,* ed. A. Owen Aldridge (Urbana: University of Illinois Press, 1971), pp. 111–40. A valuable analysis of the origins and early development of Romanticism in Spain.

SEMPERE Y GUARINOS, JUAN. *Ensayo de una biblioteca de los mejores escritores del reynado de Carlos III.* 6 vols. in 5 (Madrid: Imprenta Real, 1785–1789). Brief accounts of these writers and their works. Excellent as a contemporary commentary. There is a facsimile reprint of this work made in 1963 in three volumes by the Dolphin Book Company.

SERRANO Y SANZ, M. "Poesías y cartas inéditas de D. Juan Mcléndez Valdés," *Revue Hispanique,* 4 (1897), 266–313. Interesting information about Meléndez' early years.

SIMONDE DE SISMONDI, J. C. L. *A Historical View of the Literature of the South of Europe,* trans. Thomas Roscoe. 2 vols. (London: George Bell and Sons, 1883). Important as a Romantic commentary on eighteenth-century literature.

Index

Colford, William, 7, 21, 26, 163, 164, 165, 172
Condillac, Étienne Bonnot de, 94, 96-97, 100, 109, 119, 167
Constable, John, 73
Convento de Santo Tomás, 11, 14
Corral, Andrés del, 57
Cotarelo y Mori, Emilio, 13, 163, 164, 172
Cox, R. Merritt, 164, 165, 170, 172
Cruz, San Juan de la, 61
Cuentos y poesías más que picantes, 70
Cueto, Leopoldo Augusto de, 172

"(A) Dance," *see* "De un baile"
David, Jacques Louis, 86
Debussy, Claude, 78
"De la primavera," 64
"De las ciencias," 67, 103
"De las riquezas," 66
(El) delincuente honrado, 38
Demerson, Georges, 7, 24, 28, 38, 50, 52, 53, 100, 139, 140, 163, 164, 165, 167, 169, 170, 172
"De mis cantares," 63
"De mis deseos," 68
"Despair," *see* "(El) despecho"
"(El) despecho," 77
"(La) despedida," 71
"(La) despedida del anciano," 38, 137
"(El) deseo de gloria en los profesores de las artes," 38
"(The) Desire For Glory by Professors of the Arts," *see* "(El) deseo de gloria en los profesores de las artes"
"De un baile," 65
Discursos forenses, 7, 9, 12, 122, 127, 144-61
"Doña Elvira," 76, 85
Donoso Cortés, Juan María, 55
Don Quixote, 37, 84, 156
Don Sancho García, 17
"Dorila," 68, 69
dos de mayo, 48

"(The) Dove of Filis," *see* "(La) paloma de Filis"

(L') Embarquement Pour L'Île De Cythère, 83, 84, 85
"Emotions and Desires Felt by a Spaniard on Returning to His Homeland," *see* "Afectos y deseos de un español al volver a su patria"
"En la desgraciada muerte del Coronel Don José Cadalso," 113, 126-27
Ensayo sobre la propiedad, 39
"En un convite de amistad," 71
(Los) eruditos a la violeta, 17
Espronceda, José de, 120
Essay on Property, see Ensayo sobre la propiedad

"(The) Farewell of the Old Man," *see* "La despedida del anciano"
"Fanaticism," *see* "(El) fanatismo"
"(El) fanatismo," 108
"(The) Farewell," *see* "(La) despedida"
"(The) Farewell of the Old Man," *see* "La despedida del anciano"
fastidio universal, 114-21
Feijoo, Benito Jerónimo, 91
"(La) felicidad de la vida del campo," 24
Ferdinand VII, 47, 48, 49, 55
Fernández de Rojas, Juan, 56
fête champêtre, 80
Forner, Juan Pablo, 57, 164
Foulché-Delbosc, Raymond, 70, 163, 166, 172
Fragonard, Jean Honoré, 79
Froldi, Rinaldo, 172

García Gutiérrez, Antonio, 102
Garcilaso de la Vega, 57, 60, 71, 123
Glover, Michael, 165, 172
Godoy, Manuel, 41, 42, 44, 47, 108, 138, 139, 168, 169, 172
Góngora, Luis de, 64, 71, 89
González, Diego, 18, 56, 57, 58, 80

Index

Index